Studies in the Modern Japanese Economy

General Editors: **Malcolm Falkus**, University of New England, Armidale, New South Wales, Australia; and **Kojiro Niino**, Kobe University, Japan

An understanding of the modern Japanese economy remains both important and elusive. Its importance needs little stressing. From the 1950s Japan's economy grew at a rate unparalleled elsewhere and, despite recent setbacks, the economy remains strong and dynamic with increasing investment overseas. Indeed, Japanese-owned companies now produce more overseas than they do at home. Yet an understanding of this economic performance is made difficult by the wide cultural divide between Japanese and Western societies. On the one hand an understanding of the many unique features of Japan's economic and social life is essential if we are to appreciate the Japanese achievement, but on the other hand this very uniqueness makes communication difficult. Straightforward translations of Japanese works frequently mean little to Western readers because the underlying attitudes and assumptions are so unfamiliar.

This series has been planned in the belief that there is a need for scholarly studies on the modern Japanese economy which are written by experts (both Japanese and Western) and aimed at Western readers. Accordingly, we have planned a series of books which will explore all the major areas of Japanese economic life. The books will present up-to-date material, and, where necessary, they will place Japan in its wider international context.

Titles include:

Yujiro Hayami
JAPANESE AGRICULTURE UNDER SIEGE

Toru Iwami
JAPAN IN THE INTERNATIONAL FINANCIAL SYSTEM

Kazuo Koike
UNDERSTANDING INDUSTRIAL RELATIONS IN MODERN JAPAN

Ryōshin Minami
THE ECONOMIC DEVELOPMENT OF JAPAN (2nd edn)

Carl Mosk
COMPETITION AND COOPERATION IN JAPANESE LABOUR MARKETS

Shinji Ogura
BANKING, THE STATE AND INDUSTRIAL PROMOTION IN DEVELOPING JAPAN, 1900–73

Mitsuaki Okabe (*editor*)
THE STRUCTURE OF THE JAPANESE ECONOMY

Yoshitaka Suzuki
JAPANESE MANAGEMENT STRUCTURES, 1920–80

Toshiaki Tachibanaki
PUBLIC POLICIES AND THE JAPANESE ECONOMY
Savings, Investments, Unemployment, Inequality

Studies on the Modern Japanese Economy
Series Standing Order ISBN 0–333–71503–9
(*outside North America only*)

You can receive future titles in this series as they are published by placing a standing order. Please contact your bookseller or, in case of difficulty, write to us at the address below with your name and address, the title of the series and the ISBN quoted above.

Customer Services Department, Macmillan Distribution Ltd, Houndmills, Basingstoke, Hampshire RG21 6XS, England

Banking, the State and Industrial Promotion in Developing Japan, 1900–73

Shinji Ogura
Professor of Economics
Chiba University of Commerce
Japan

palgrave

First published 2002 by
PALGRAVE
Houndmills, Basingstoke, Hampshire RG21 6XS and
175 Fifth Avenue, New York, N.Y. 10010
Companies and representatives throughout the world

PALGRAVE is the new global academic imprint of
St. Martin's Press LLC Scholarly and Reference Division and
Palgrave Publishers Ltd (formerly Macmillan Press Ltd).

ISBN 0–333–71139–4

This book is printed on paper suitable for recycling and made from fully managed and sustained forest sources.

A catalogue record for this book is available from the British Library.

A catalogue record for this book is available from the Library of Congress.

10 9 8 7 6 5 4 3 2 1
11 10 09 08 07 06 05 04 03 02

Printed and bound in Great Britain by
Antony Rowe Ltd, Chippenham, Wiltshire

Contents

List of Tables

Preface

Japan's corporate groupings are currently the focus of much interest, and recent advances in research, particularly into Japan's main bank system, reflect that surge of interest. There has been an especially strong tendency to re-evaluate the role and function of Japan's commercial banks in these corporate groupings.[1]

In this work I use the term 'main bank' to denote a bank that is not necessarily a company's largest creditor by volume but is ready to act as lender of last resort when it faces difficulty, and 'main creditor' to denote a company's largest lender by volume.[2] The former should be clearly discriminated from the latter, although there is no doubt that banks are eager to act as lender of last resort in the hope of eventually acquiring the status of main creditor. In fact there have been a number of cases where a main bank has endured somewhat disappointing transactions as part of its long-term aim to become a company's main creditor.

In advanced countries banks have done as much as major industries to shape the financial architecture and economic system. In Japan the main banks of the corporate groupings have enjoyed great influence over, and have sometimes had to take considerable responsibility for, the managerial policy and funding position of their customers. Commercial banks have had to develop the kind of banking services their main customers require to keep their customers' and their own fund positions healthy. They have also had to learn to screen applicants for loans quickly and correctly.

With regard to main bank status, the prewar banks that were responsible for the banking affairs of zaibatsu-affiliated enterprises and the postwar banks heading corporate groups may appear to be alike, but in reality they are quite different. Strictly speaking the former did not qualify as main banks because they were completely under the control of the zaibatsu families and could not exercize their own discretion. They had little interest in exercising influence over the managerial policy and fund position of their customers, and consequently had no need to develop a long-term lending business (although they were required to meet the demand for long-term capital loans by zaibatsu-affiliated companies, electric power companies and so on). Instead they concentrated on providing short-term loans, discounting commercial bills and handling foreign bills of exchange.

This was especially true of Mitsui Bank, which stuck to the conservative lending policy it had established before World War I. Mitsui, which was ambitious to become a genuine commercial bank, remained faithful to the principle that the discounting of bills was preferable to loaning on bills and that short-term lending was preferable to long-term lending. In putting this principle into practice, it attached great importance both to foreign exchange business with trading companies such as Mitsui and Company and to offering securities services to debtor customers.

In the 1930s the major banks began the transition from being in-house banks of the zaibatsu to acting as main banks. After the out-break of war between Japan and China in 1937 it became urgent for the commercial banks to meet the demand for long-term capital funds by their customers in the munitions industry. However, when their funds ran short and their debts increased to the Bank of Japan the banks had to depend heavily on the Industrial Bank of Japan and other government financial institutions specializing in long-term loans. Eventually they were forced to return mainly to short-term lending. Much the same happened after World War II.

Fortunately, from these bitter experiences they learnt how to use specialist government financial institutions both to meet their customers' demands for long-term loans and to resolve their fund shortage problems. They also learnt that such business could serve as a substitute for their securities business by restricting the average loan term – they had been prohibited from underwriting corporate securities by a Securities and Exchange Law passed just after the war.

A banking and financial system based on specialization and differentiated roles had been firmly established by the late 1950s, when corporate groupings emerged. One of the most important means available to banks for promoting corporate groupings was to offer long-term loans to all their important customers, but this was impossible as they had insufficient funds. Instead they reintroduced the sectoral loan prioritization system that had prevailed during the wartime economy and set up cross-shareholdings among their best customers.

In the late 1960s they became deeply dissatisfied with their heavy dependence on long-term credit banks and government financial institutions because this was forcing them to accept government interference in their lending activities. Their headlong dash to free themselves of this predicament and become universal banks caused the bubble economy of the late 1980s.

In closing, a word about the material upon which this book is based. Information on the lending activities of Mitsui Bank and Teikoku Bank before the end of World War II was provided to me by Sakura Bank, while information on Mitsui Bank's lending between 1950 and 1960 was provided by a former executive of that bank and others. Regrettably, data for the period since 1961 has not been released and I have had to use what information is available in the banks' officially published histories.

SHINJI OGURA

Acknowledgements

My deepest thanks go to a number of former executives of Mitsui Bank (now the Sumitomo Mitsui Banking Corporation) who kindly gave me access to the documents that substantiate this study but asked for their names to be withheld.

I am especially grateful for the assistance of Akinobu Otani, whose invaluable work as an archivist at the Mitsui Bank Research Division has helped to ensure that scholars are able accurately to trace the bank's history. I am also, of course, indebted to his colleagues at the Research Division.

I very much appreciate the cooperation of Kaoru Sugihara (Osaka University), Janet Hunter (London School of Economics and Political Science) and Costas Lapavitsas (SOAS, University of London), who in 1994–95, during my stay in London as an academic visitor to the SOAS, made constructive comments on the draft, upon which Chapter 5 of this book is based.

I am extremely thankful to Professor Malcolm Falkus (University of New England, Australia), T. M. Farmiloe and Yoshimaru Tadokoro for providing me with the opportunity to publish this book. To turn a Japanese draft into an English book requires a great deal of effort. Professor Falkus read the final draft and checked it from an editorial viewpoint, while Peter Poole-Wilson checked my translation from Japanese into English – I cannot thank him enough for his invaluable advice.

I am also indebted to Professors Sadayuki Sato, Shigeru Tanase, Satoshi Yamazaki, Go Tian-Kang and Jun Ikegami for encouraging me, as my academic advisers, to undertake this study.

I would like to thank friends and colleagues for their comments and suggestions, including Makoto Kasuya, Mitsunori Amano, Yoichi Kumaoka, Makoto Kojima, Hisahiko Saito, Masaaki Shimizu, Soichi Takeuchi, Hisatomi Naruse, Kyuji Yoshikawa, James Baldwin, Warren Elliot, Stephen Cullis and Robert Davies.

Finally I am grateful to my family, whose speedy word-processing afforded me more time to improve the book's contents.

SHINJI OGURA

Introduction: Analytical Issues

This book examines when and how Japan's largest banks changed from establishments responsible for the banking affairs of zaibatsu-affiliated enterprises into commercial banks responsible for the banking affairs of major companies in all sectors of the economy. Mitsui Bank has been chosen as a case study. The emphasis will be on its lending policy, managerial organization and business transactions. This is because Mitsui Bank could not have become responsible for the banking affairs of major companies without establishing a lending policy based on close relationships with these companies and the managerial organization necessary for putting this policy into practice.

The analytical method used in this book is to an extent based on that established by leading business historians. While influential academics have made remarkable theoretical contributions to the subject of business history they do not seem to have shown much interest in the case history of commercial banks. In general, in Japan most economic historians have tended to focus on banks' business transactions, while most business historians and the writers of official bank histories have tended to focus on managerial organization. Very few have paid attention to banks' lending policies. As a result there have been no analyses of banks' lending policies and managerial organization based on analysis of their business transactions.

In order to draw general conclusions about the relationship between lending policies, managerial organization and business transactions it is essential to study information and data on as many major commercial banks as possible. However it is quite difficult to do so because most banks' documents on activities such as lending are unavailable to outsiders. Mitsui Bank is exceptional in this respect as documents on its activities are available to academics, which is why Mitsui has been chosen as the exemplar.

When conducting research on the subject special attention has to be paid to the following: the process of examining loan applications, particularly, in respect of which members of the department concerned, including the managing director, plays the most important role in examining individual loan applications: the result of lending, for example whether or not the loans are repaid; and the vital relationship between a bank's available funds and the extent of its lending.

As noted above, business historians have tended to neglect banks' lending policies. For example, while Alfred Chandler and Hidemasa Morikawa have made remarkable contributions to the study of business history (and from whom I have learned much about conducting case studies), it seems they have reflected little on major banks' role in the functioning of industrial enterprises. In theory, case histories of major banks and their relationship with industrial enterprises are separate subjects, but in practice the two tend to be inseparable, with the conclusions drawn from the former informing the latter.

Chandler accepts that investment bankers first appeared on the boards of US industrial firms during the merger movement at the turn of the twentieth century.[1] However he discriminates between the US and British investment-banking firms of the time, consisting of little more than a few partners with a tiny secretarial staff, and the large German banks with a substantial number of employees, including specialists responsible for the banks' relationship with major industrial firms.[2] According to Chandler, German industry provides the best and only true example of financial capitalism:[3]

> The relationship of the promoters and even the investment bankers to the merged enterprises on whose boards they sat remained, like that of the venture capitalists, more personal than institutional. Even the largest incorporated investment banks – such as those of James Stillman and George F. Baker – were still operated like the house of Morgan, the most respected and most powerful of them all: that is, they were personally run enterprises with small staffs. Their structure and functions were very different from those of the German 'great banks' that played such a significant role in the financing of modern German industrial enterprises. They were more like the large British merchant banks, which, however, played only a small part in the financing of British industry. The representatives of the American banks on the boards of the newly consolidated American industrial enterprises had little personal knowledge of the businesses they had helped to finance, and they continued to rely almost wholly on

the managers of each economy for essential information on the company's internal affairs and its external challenges and opportunities. Therefore, as the knowledge and experience of the full-time managers on the board increased and the new enterprise succeeded in financing its current operations and long-term growth primarily from retained earnings, the influence of the financiers waned.[4]

In my opinion Chandler pays too much attention to investment bankers and too little to the development of modern commercial banks in the US.

Likewise Morikawa refutes that banks played an important role in the formation of the Japanese zaibatsu (groups of diversified businesses, each owned by a single family):

> Among the variables that affected the ability of the zaibatsu to implement diversification strategies during the years 1893–1913 were managerial resources, organizational structures, and the zaibatsu family as owner and controller. I will attempt to counter the view common among zaibatsu historians in Japan that the zaibatsu developed by relying on their wealth of funds, especially the financial resources of their banks.[5]

He makes a similar criticism of Japanese academics who have focused on the financial ties in the zaibatsu multisubsidiary system that came into being after World War I:

> The study of the zaibatsu multi-subsidiary system has flourished since before the Second World War, but almost all works have focused on the financial ties among the constituent enterprises or on the concentration of capital and oligopolization. They have not treated such important management-related issues as the nature and degree of control exercised by the head office over the subsidiaries or by the owner family over the salaried managers.[6]

Interestingly, he draws his negative conclusions from detailed observations of Mitsui Bank:

> The zaibatsu with banks were cautious ... in using their own banks. For a zaibatsu to sink its deposits into its enterprises

and then to be unable to recover them would do devastating damage not only to the reputation of the bank but also to the family's honor. Reflecting the zaibatsu families' fear of this outcome, the zaibatsu with banks avoided as much as possible investing their bank's funds in their own enterprises, a restraint that became particularly marked after 1900.

The Mitsui zaibatsu provided the classic example of the practice. During Nakamigawa Hikojiro's promotion of industrial investments by Mitsui, the lending policy of Mitsui Bank was to give preferential treatment regarding terms of lending limits and interest rates to the Mitsui subsidiaries. Consequently, at the end of June 1899 enterprises within the Mitsui zaibatsu accounted for 87 per cent of the overdrafts on current accounts at the bank's head office. In order to counteract this development, after Nakamigawa's death Mitsui adopted a policy of maximum regulation of lending by its bank to Mitsui subsidiaries. The policy went so far as to require that Mitsui Bank hold down increases in deposits themselves. As Masuda, executive director of the Mitsui head office, put it at a meeting of Mitsui Bank branch managers in 1904: 'Deposits should be kept from growing, insofar as possible without offending customers. Funds should be safely tied up in loans without becoming uncollectable, even at low interest rates.' This policy had been adopted, he explained, in response to outside criticism that 'Mitsui is accepting deposits from others and operating a variety of its own enterprises. It is, however, extremely unsound and improper for it to invest in its own enterprises funds received on deposits from others.' As a result, conflicts concerning deposit increases often occurred between the negative policy of the Mitsui Bank head office and the aggressive policy of the branches.

It is commonly argued that the zaibatsu operated banks only as a means of getting their hands on the copious funds for diversification. That argument holds for a certain period in the development of the zaibatsu banks, but, as the experience of Mitsui after Nakamigawa illustrates, it would be highly erroneous to fix upon this as a general explanation of the zaibatsu–bank relationship.[7]

Thus Morikawa seems to have almost the same view as Chandler on banks' role in industry. In this regard Mitsui Bank under Nakamigawa can be equated with the house of Morgan (the most powerful investment banker at the turn of the twentieth century in the US) and Mitsui's own enterprises with the US industrial enterprises; and Mitsui Bank under Masuda can be equated with American financiers whose influence had waned.

SHINJI OGURA

1
Mitsui Bank under the Control of the Mitsui Family, 1876–1929

Today's major commercial banks were originally the in-house banks of zaibatsu and were responsible for the banking affairs of all zaibatsu-affiliated enterprises in prewar Japan. Mitsui Bank was the largest of these banks and the nucleus of the diverse businesses owned by the Mitsui family.

In the 1890s the bank, under the guidance of Hikojiro Nakamigawa (1854–1901, a graduate of Keio Gijuku – now Keio University – and nephew of the educator Yukichi Fukuzawa), switched to a particularly progressive policy of building closer relationships with industry in order first to gain control of leading companies through loans and then bring them into the Mitsui group. This policy was suddenly abandoned during the recession of 1900–1 because the bank was on the verge of being forced into suspending payments as a result of the policy. Ultimately the bank escaped bankruptcy by asking the Bank of Japan for help and adopting sounder policies, such as regulating the increase of loans and selecting its loan clientele more carefully.

The bank's financial distress so shocked the Mitsuis that they decided to withdraw from the commercial banking business, but had the bank's progressive policies succeeded Mitsui's rivals, such as Mitsubishi and Sumitomo, would have copied Mitsui and made their banks the nucleus of all zaibatsu-related business.

The early years of Mitsui Bank

The Meiji Restoration and the establishment of the bank in 1876

Mitsui Bank was established as the first private bank in Japan in 1876, nine years after the fall of the Tokugawa regime. Its origins can be traced back to when Hachirobei Takatoshi Mitsui opened a money-exchange shop in Edo (now Tokyo) in 1683. One of the most important tasks of the new government that replaced the Tokugawa Shogunate in the Meiji Restoration in 1868 was to build a firm currency and banking system. In 1871 the government introduced a new currency system based on the gold standard and the yen replaced the ryo. However gold and silver bimetallism rather than the gold standard took root in the economy as the government was in dire financial straits. It was not until 1897 that the government managed to establish the gold standard completely.

In 1872 the government promulgated the National Bank Act (*Kokuritsu Ginko Jorei*). Previously there had been a clash of opinions within the government between the advocates of a British-type banking system based on a central bank and the advocates of an American-type banking system based on national banks. Mitsui supported the former, which prevailed at first, but eventually the latter gained the upper hand. Under the Act four newly chartered national banks were empowered by the government to issue convertible bank notes that could be exchanged for non-convertible government notes, a flood of which was a serious problem confronting the new government.

Prior to this choice of national banking system, of the families that had made a formal application to establish a private bank, immediate permission had been granted only to the Mitsuis and the Ono family, influential merchants since the early Edo period and one of the Meiji government's three fiscal agents (the other two being the Mitsui and Shimada families). The latter bank collapsed at the end of the nineteenth century. Upon the introduction of the new system the government not only revoked these permits but also prohibited the use of the word *ginko* (bank) by financial institutions other than national banks.

Reluctantly acceding to the government's pressure to establish a joint-venture bank under the Act, the Mitsuis founded the Mitsui–Ono Kumiai Bank with the Ono family in 1872. Next year the government officially named the bank Dai-Ichi (First) National Bank, the first of its kind in Japan. Two years later the Mitsuis tried again to establish a bank of their own and submitted a new application to the government. The government eventually approved their application by amending certain provisions of the National Bank Act. Thus Mitsui Bank was established.

In 1882 a central bank, the Bank of Japan, was established as the sole bank entitled to issue convertible bank notes. Consequently in 1883 the approximately 150 national banks that existed at that time were deprived of the authority to issue bank notes and to handle Treasury accounts. One hundred and twenty two national banks were reorganized as private banks after the Bank Act (*Ginko Jorei*) came into force. The number of commercial banks subsequently began to increase, and by 1901 there were over 1800, the sharp increase in number being a result of the boom that followed the cessation of the Sino-Japanese War. In 1895 Mitsubishi Bank and Sumitomo Bank were established and in 1896 the Dai-Ichi National Bank, in which Mitsui still had a stake, was renamed the Dai-Ichi Bank. These three banks plus Yasuda Bank (established in 1880 and today called Fuji Bank), and Mitsui Bank became the nation's five major banks in the second half of the 1890s.

The government pursued a policy of encouraging the merger of small private banks in order to strengthen the commercial banking system, and various specialist banks were set up to handle foreign exchange and long-term industrial loans. By about 1900 the essential structure of Japan's banking system had been established.[1]

Mitsui Bank reforms in the 1890s

During the last decade of the nineteenth century, when the number of Japanese banks increased rapidly, Mitsui Bank underwent modernization reform at the hands of Hikojiro Nakamigawa, himself under the command of Kaoru Inoue (1835–1915), the Mitsui family's main outside adviser. Inoue, a Meiji Restoration leader and an influential politician in the Meiji regime, was entrusted by the family with almost full power to direct the Mitsui-affiliated companies without assuming any formal position in them. Nakamigawa held the positions of director, deputy president and executive director of the bank between 1891 and 1901. It was to rectify the bank's severe financial problems, starting in 1890, that Inoue appointed Nakamigawa.

Mitsui Bank faced a run on its Kyoto branch during the first recession of the capitalist system after the Meiji Restoration. *The Mitsui Bank: A History of the First 100 Years* (1976), the bank's official history, says the following about Inoue's contribution to the reform of the bank:

> Inoue had known Nakamigawa for many years and urged him to join Mitsui to conduct its modernization reforms. ... Nakamigawa conceived a grand plan for reforming The Mitsui Bank. It called for bad loans, reorganizing the Bank's internal structure, and replacing the Bank's government largesse with a new image of it as a modern financial institution working closely with industry. The Bank had to sever old ties with the government. It was to become, eventually, the financial institution responsible for the banking affairs of all Mitsui enterprises.[2]

This official description of Nakamigawa's contribution postdated that in *The 80 Year History of Mitsui Bank* (1957). The latter fully evaluated his contribution, which previously had been neglected. Unfortunately, while trying to be faithful to the historical facts these official histories nonetheless seem to have overestimated that contribution.

A careful reading of these histories reveals that Nakamigawa deviated completely from the sound banking principles that the bank was required to observe as a commercial bank. He performed remarkably both in redeeming bad debts (the first phase of his reform plan) and in reorganizing the bank's internal structure (the second phase of the plan), but deviated from good practice during the third phase of his reform plan:

> Nakamigawa's internal reform of The Mitsui Bank facilitated the third phase of his reform plan – building a closer relationship between the Bank and industry. With internal reform completed, the Bank was no longer an old-fashioned institution. Its business operations were now more modern than those of all other banks, and its new structure proved most advantageous for the industrial expansion of the Mitsui group. Nakamigawa worked hard to develop Japanese industry after bringing many companies into the Mitsui group. These companies were in three categories. First were those that came under Mitsui's control because of defaulted loans. ... In the second category were companies in which The Mitsui Bank had an interest and took steps to acquire. ... The Mitsui Bank gained control of companies in these two categories

through loans. In the third category were former state-run companies which the Bank purchased from the government, such as
silk-reeling mills. Mitsui placed all these companies under the
control of its Industrial Department, attached directly to the
Mitsui Motokata.[3]

A few pages later it is suggested that the lending policy he adopted
during the third phase of the reforms was not suitable for the bank:
'The industries Nakamigawa had brought into Mitsui, particularly
Kanegafuchi, Oji Paper and Tanaka Seizosho, performed quite poorly
during 1900 and 1901, and loans to them became burdensome for
The Mitsui Bank'.[4] Although Mitsui Bank made progress as a commercial bank after Nakamigawa's death in 1901, it is clear that this
progress was due to the internal reforms conducted during the second
phase of Nakamigawa's grand plan, as will be discussed later.

Every miller draws water to his own mill, a proverb says, and the
ambiguous accounts related in the official histories have left room
for one-sided interpretations by some business historians. Even
Hidemasa Morikawa overestimates Nakamigawa's contribution to
Mitsui Bank's reform, and suggests a reason for Nakamigawa's fall
from grace:

> After Nakamigawa's death, Masuda became senior executive
> director (*senmu riji*) of the Management Department of the
> Secretariat of the Mitsui Family Council (*Dozokukai Jimukyoku
> Kanribu*), a body established in 1902 to exercise overall the Mitsui
> family enterprises. Masuda redirected the Mitsui zaibatsu away
> from the industrialization program of Nakamigawa's day. These
> moves can be summarized as a transformation in terms of Mitsui
> zaibatsu's business strategy from 'Industrial Mitsui' to 'Commercial
> Mitsui'.[5]

I disagree with Morikawa in that his judgement of Nakamigawa's
policy is not based on whether sound banking principles were
adhered to by Nakamigawa, but on whether Nakamigawa's choice of
zaibatsu business strategy was proper. The undeniable fact is that
Nakamigawa fell from grace not because of the change of zaibatsu
business strategy from 'industrial Mitsui' to 'commercial Mitsui', but
because he failed to rehabilitate the bank. Morikawa also tends to

exaggerate Nakamigawa's academic career, character and credentials. He depicts Nakamigawa as a highly educated person with courage, foresight and determination, and as a pioneer who used many college-educated people to carry out his industrialization plan:

> Nakamigawa intended to use college-educated men in rebuilding Mitsui Bank and carrying out his industrialization policy and accordingly hired, at high salaries, many Keio graduates. Most were hired after gaining experience elsewhere rather than immediately after leaving Keio. For Nakamigawa, the use of a large number of university graduates was an important element in Mitsui's reform, but the introduction of so many Keio graduates stimulated criticism of Nakamigawa within Mitsui for having a 'Keio clique'.[6]

Strictly speaking the men recruited by Nakamigawa were not university graduates but college ones, because it was not until 1920 that Keio was formally raised to the status of a university. In addition, Nakamigawa's introduction of so many Keio graduates should be regarded as a shortcoming in his personnel policy rather than carelessness, stimulating criticism of himself.

On the verge of bankruptcy

Runs on deposits

It was Takashi Masuda (1848–1938), executive director of Mitsui and Company and a member of the Mitsui Family Council (*Mitsuike Dozokukai*), who finally succeeded in rebuilding Mitsui Bank, based on the sound banking principles from which Nakamigawa had deviated.

Masuda joined Mitsui in 1876 when Mitsui and Company was established. By then he already possessed considerable experience in foreign trade, and after the Meiji Restoration he had come to Inoue's attention and had been hired as deputy director of the Mint Bureau in the Ministry of Finance. As president of the newly formed Mitsui and Company he devoted himself to developing a workforce that was rich in knowledge, experience and international trade ability. He hired many graduates of the Tokyo Higher Commercial College

(Tokyo Koto Shogyo Gakko, now Hitotsubashi University) and its predecessors, such as the Commercial Training School (Shoho Koshusho).[7]

The economic boom that followed the Sino-Japanese War of 1894–95 ended in 1900 when a depression in the United States and the Boxer Rebellion affected Japan. Unfortunately some of the companies that had been brought into Mitsui by Nakamigawa, such as Kanegafuchi, Oji Paper and Tanaka Seizosho, performed quite poorly during 1900–1, and loans to them became burdensome for Mitsui Bank, as noted above. Moreover in April 1900 a small daily newspaper, the *Niroku Shimpo*, carried a number of articles attacking the bank, particularly the policies of Nakamigawa, and these articles caused runs on several branches of the bank.[8]

Although the bank ultimately managed to avoid the suspension of payments, commercial banking proved an unviable business for Mitsui after the *Niroku Shimpo* incident. Masuda gradually increased his influence within Mitsui, winning the confidence of Kaoru Inoue and overseeing Mitsui Bank's operations, in place of Nakamigawa.[9] During the incident a written pledge had been exchanged between the Mitsui Family Council and the bank that prior consultation would be sought on all important questions affecting the bank. This requirement had also been written into the newly enacted Family constitution (*Mitsuike Kaken*) and it had caused Nakamigawa to lose his influence.[10] After Nakamigawa's death from illness in 1901, Masuda acquired greater power in Mitsui than Nakamigawa had enjoyed at the height of his career. Masuda began to exercise great influence over Mitsui Bank, although he did not assume its top position.

In 1902 Masuda added a control department (*Kanribu*) to the zaibatsu's administrative structure. (With the promotion of Nakamigawa, in 1893 Mitsui Bank, Mitsui and Company, Mitsui Mining and Mitsui Dry Goods Shop had been reorganized into unlimited partnerships and the Mitsui Family Council – the central governing body of the family's businesses – had been established a little later.) Then Masuda recommended a new lending policy, whereby the bank would keep at arm's length the companies to which it provided loans.[11] In addition the bank was demoted to a lower rank in the Mitsui group and Mitsui and Company took its place as the nucleus of the group. By engaging in arm's length transactions with its customers, sometimes even with zaibatsu affiliates, the bank aimed to become a genuine commercial bank.

Nakamigawa's successor as top executive of Mitsui Bank was Senkichiro Hayakawa (1863–1922), the bank's executive director from 1901 to 1909 and head of managing directors from 1909 to 1918. Hayakawa had entered the Ministry of Finance after graduating from Tokyo Imperial University (now the University of Tokyo), and subsequently joined Mitsui on the recommendation of Kaoru Inoue. Prior to entering the bank he had become a member of the Mitsui Family Council. He was appointed with the expectation that he would implement the ideas of Inoue and Masuda. A soft-spoken man, he was particularly adept at handling personnel problems.[12]

Nakamigawa had already established detailed regulations for loan procedures and started to improve the coordination of the operations of the bank's branches and offices with the operations of the head office. He had also tried to improve the individual operations of each branch, to widen the exchange of information between head office and the branches and to clarify the scope of responsibility of each branch.[13] The changes made by Nakamigawa were retained by the bank under Masuda's supervision for the time being.

Strangely enough it was not Hayakawa but Seihin Ikeda (1867–1950) – Japan's most influential banker and a well-known public financier, Mitsui Bank's managing director from 1909 to 1933 and head of managing directors from 1918 to 1933, governor of the Bank of Japan and Minister of Finance from 1937 to 1938 – who held real power over the bank's operations, particularly with regard to the examination of loan applications by major borrowers and the overall management of funds at the start of Masuda's reforms. Ikeda, who had studied at Harvard University after graduating from Keio Gijuku, had joined the bank in 1895 and in 1900, at the age of 32, had become deputy general manager of the business department at the head office and manager of the loan section of that department. As Nakamigawa's son-in-law he had been a member of the 'Keio clique', but had managed to survive this disadvantage after the downfall of Nakamigawa.

Ikeda won Masuda's favour not only because Hayakawa lacked business experience and had no interest in the bank's operations, apart from handling personnel problems, but also because the general manager of the business department (a former policeman without business experience) had entrusted the department's operations to

Ikeda. It is certain that Ikeda was an excellent bank employee, and it is even more certain that he would not have gained real power over the bank's operations if the bank had developed itself fully as a modern commercial bank with an efficient head office. That is, Ikeda's power reflected the lack of development of the bank's head office, which prevented it from functioning effectively as the main branch of the network.

The planned withdrawal from commercial banking

Mitsui's various businesses advanced in leaps and bounds during the Russo-Japanese War of 1904–5 and made the Mitsui family one of the richest in the world. After the war Inoue and Masuda took the drastic step of advising the Mitsui family to withdraw from the management of Mitsui Bank and thus avoid the risks inherent in the commercial banking business.

Inoue and Masuda's plan was aimed at making the Mitsui family great financiers like the Rothschilds and the Morgans by establishing a new (non-commercial banking) financial institution to succeed Mitsui Bank. In 1907 Masuda, accompanied by three representatives of Mitsui Bank, duly left for Europe and the United States, ostensibly to survey organizational and business aspects of European and American banks. However the real purpose of the tour was to make preparations for the withdrawal of the Mitsui family from management of the bank rather than to make recommendations for the bank's reform.

As a result of the tour Inoue and Masuda dropped their plan, although in 1909 Mitsui Bank was changed from an unlimited partnership to a joint-stock company, capitalized at 12 million yen by the Mitsui Family Council.[14] If the plan had not been cancelled the new financial institution would have become the financing arm of Mitsui Gomei, a holding company that included the Mitsui Family Council's control department, which would have developed various types of investment banking business, including securities.

Mitsui and Company's support for the rehabilitation of the bank

The abandonment of the plan meant that Mitsui Bank, now a joint-stock company, was able to keep its commercial banking business.

Furthermore it would be responsible for developing securities business and other types of investment banking.

Roughly speaking, Mitsui and Company's rescue of Mitsui Bank had two purposes. One was to help Mitsui Bank to establish new ventures, such as a foreign exchange business. The other was to gain control of companies such as Oji Paper and shore them up to help Mitsui Bank retrieve its bad debts. The bank underwrote foreign currency bonds for the first time in 1909. The bonds in question were municipal bonds of the city of Kyoto, worth 45 million francs.[15] (This operation was originally planned as a rehearsal for the new financial business the Mitsui family would pursue after the abolition of Mitsui Bank.) Under Masuda's guidance the bank followed the instructions of Senjiro Watanabe – a director of Mitsui and Company and a manager at its London Branch – in preparing the operation.[16] (Masuda had retired from Mitsui after the incorporation of the control department of the Family Council into Mitsui Gomei in 1909. However he maintained great influence as an adviser to Mitsui Gomei and still wanted Mitsui Bank to increase its earning power in order to complete its rehabilitation.)

Mitsui Bank was in a good position to develop a foreign exchange business as Mitsui and Company was a member of the Mitsui group. Nonetheless the bank hesitated to enter the foreign exchange business until it was forced to establish a foreign department under the strict orders of Masuda in 1913.[17] Kiichiro Sato (1894–1974, president of Teikoku Bank and Mitsui Bank from 1946 to 1959 and a dominant leader of the postwar Mitsui group) wrote in his memoirs that Mitsui and Company taught Mitsui Bank how to conduct foreign exchange business and that this business proved to be extremely high-yielding.[18] The bank was able to advance more quickly than other commercial banks in this respect because of its close relationship with Mitsui and Company, for example the Yokohama branch of the company helped the bank to purchase export bills for raw silk sold to the US and Europe, and the London branch, the New York branch and the cotton department of the company helped the bank to settle import bills for US and Indian cotton imported to Japan.[19]

In a move indirectly aimed at helping Mitsui Bank to wipe out its bad debts, Mitsui and Company gained control of the companies in which the bank had a controlling stake through loans.

The bank had gained control of Oji Paper in 1896 but later its loans to this company went sour. In the 1900s the company was managed by a succession of executives dispatched by the bank to rehabilitate it. In 1911 serious problems arose with regard to the election of Oji executives. When the company's executives resigned en masse, Mitsui and Company sent Ginjiro Fujiyama, general manager of its lumber department and Otaru Branch, to Oji as its executive managing director at the demand of Inoue and Masuda.[20] Two years later the bank was able to redeem its outstanding loans to Oji Paper with the proceeds reaped from the sale of the company's bonds in London.[21]

Mitsui and Company played an even more significant role in helping the Shibaura Works to repay its bad debt to Mitsui Bank. The Mitsui Family Council reorganized Shibaura into a joint-stock company, capitalized at one million yen in 1904. Moreover in 1909 it turned Shibaura into a Japanese–American joint venture, importing technological know-how and capital from General Electric in the US, for whom Mitsui and Company acted as import agent in Japan. After that Shibaura's business improved quickly and substantially, its capital increasing to 20 million yen by 1920.

As a matter of course Mitsui and Company also secured the necessary trading rights for raw materials and manufactured products from the companies concerned.[22]

Traders as preferred borrowers

When World War I broke out in 1914, foreign trade was stopped and the Japanese economy fell into chaos. In 1915, however, exports increased sharply and the total foreign trade balance had reached a favourable 1.4 billion yen by 1918.[23]

Domestic enterprises, especially trading companies, enjoyed wartime prosperity, and Mitsui-affiliated companies such as Kanegafuchi and Oji Paper developed into top-ranking firms. Their bad debt problem, about which Mitsui Bank had worried for a long time, was completely resolved. The bank moved into new areas of business to secure prosperous customers as its major borrowers, resulting in a sharp increase in deposits and the resolution of its bad debt problem during the wartime boom. The bank's main objective at the time was to secure prominent trading companies as major borrowers, and to expand its foreign exchange business for trading companies. Needless to say the bank's special relationship with Mitsui and Company was the motivation for this move.

Attention should be paid to the criterion Masuda emphasized for the selection of loan clientele. This clientele should be a group of major borrowers in the same trade, allowing the bank to engage in exclusive transactions with them.[24] Such companies, which became the bank's main borrowers, soon began a life or death struggle with each other for market share. Some of them ran into financial difficulty, causing the bank another serious bad debt problem towards the end of the 1920s.

Mitsui and Company increased the scale of its operations enormously during World War I and became an unrivalled giant among the country's trading companies, accounting for about 20 per cent of the total value of Japan's imports and exports. The scale of Mitsui Bank's transactions with Mitsui and Company increased proportionately. The total amount of credit extended to the company, including trade financing, had reached about 60 million yen by the end of World War I, making it the bank's major borrower. Before World War I the company had not required large loans despite being the bank's highest priority borrower, except during depressed economic conditions.[25] The total credit granted by the bank to the company amounted to about 36 million yen at the end of October 1917 and about 60 million yen at the end of April 1918, or 17 per cent and 25 per cent of the bank's credit balance at the end of December 1917 and June 1918 respectively, after taking account of the two organizations' different accounting periods.[26]

The Mitsui zaibatsu was forced to reform the bank's lending policy before and after World War I. Until then the bank had followed a strict policy of collecting stable funds at low interest rates and lending them to reliable business customers. This policy, which Inoue and Masuda had forced the bank to adopt, had been very effective in improving the bank's business during depressed times, but had caused business to stagnate during the prosperous years of the war.[27]

Two measures were taken. One was to allow the bank to reverse its sound lending policy and take positive steps to increase deposits and loans. The other was to make the bank more independent of Mitsui Gomei control by allowing it to offer 300 000 of 800 000 new shares to the public and transferring power to a newly established board of managing directors. A system in which a holding company with diverse businesses had control over a financial institution was unreasonable in essence, and became more and more anachronistic as time went on.[28]

Disclosure of the Vickers scandal (certain officials of Japan's Naval Ministry were charged with taking bribes not only from Vickers, for which Mitsui was exclusive agent, but also from Siemens-Shuckert) caused difficulties for Mitsui and Company: three top-ranking executives were arrested for bribery. In addition, after the armistice in 1918 the company suffered heavy losses from its soya bean transactions with the Dalian market in China.

These events had an adverse effect on Mitsui Bank as one of the businesses under the Mitsui Gomei's control. Combined with the bank's prewar, prereform policy of not taking positive steps to increase deposits and loans, they were a major factor in the decline of the bank's competitiveness in securing deposits. The bank yielded its top commercial bank position in deposits to Dai-Ichi Bank in 1917, and was caught up by Sumitomo Bank at about the same time.

Among the zaibatsu-affiliated banks it was Sumitomo Bank that pioneered the way to modern commercial banking by offering new shares to the public. Sumitomo Bank was established in 1895, 19 years after Mitsui Bank, and was reorganized into a joint-stock company with authorized capital of 15 million yen in 1912, three years later than Mitsui Bank. But it was ahead of Mitsui Bank by two years in offering 30 000 of 150 000 new shares to the public in 1917.

Within a year of the sale of the shares Sumitomo Bank increased the number of its managing directors from one to four, chose an outside director from among its major shareholders and established a board of managing directors with broad authority over decision making. By the spring of 1918 the bank had divided its head office into personnel, domestic, general accounting and financing, administration, research and business departments. This suggests that in those days the creditworthiness of a bank had more effect on the bank as an institution than did its owner.[29]

Mitsui Bank increased its authorized capital from 20 million yen to 100 million yen in 1919 and offered 300 000 of 800 000 new 100-yen nominal shares to the public. More than 70 per cent of the 300 000 shares were concentrated among 55 people, to whom 1000 or more shares were allocated. Although this did little to arrest depositors' fears about the bank's undercapitalization or enhance the bank's prestige in the eyes of the public, the share offering was very effective in making the bank more independent of Mitsui Gomei control. According to Tomozo Toyama (a former director of the bank), prior to 1919 if the bank was planning a new branch even construction materials such as drainpipes and gutters were subject to the Mitsui Gomei's approval.[30]

It was not until September 1919 that Mitsui Bank's three managing directors were given decision-making power, even though the directorships and the division of duties among them had come into being as far back as 1909. The lack of such power had prevented the establishment of a board of managing directors, and in those days, a head office supervised firmly and effectively by a board of managing directors was vital to a bank's supremacy over industrial enterprises.

This new power, however, did not extend to the appointment of new directors. According to Hirokichi Kamejima (the director in charge of personnel from 1923–31), even after the ties between the Mitsui Gomei and Mitsui Bank had been loosened, the Mitsui Gomei or the Mitsui family still exerted great influence over the appointment of new bank directors.[31]

Senkichiro Hayakawa (Mitsui Bank's top managing director) resigned from the bank to become vice-president of the Mitsui Gomei in 1918 and was succeeded by Seihin Ikeda, who continued to enjoy real power over loan applications by the bank's major borrowers and over the management of its fund position.

The bank increased its number of managing directors from three to four in 1919, and in 1921 strengthened its head office. The latter now consisted of six departments supervised by the four managing directors: the foreign and research departments were supervised by Seihin Ikeda, the domestic department by Naojiro Kikumoto, the administration and inspection departments by Hirokichi Kamejima, and the general accounting and financing department by Rikisaburo Imai.[32]

Mitsui Bank had regained its leading position among Japan's major banks by the end of 1924, when it created a foreign exchange department at the head office to take charge of the bank's foreign exchange business – the foreign department remained in control of foreign relations in general. At that time the bank operated 23 establishments: the head office business department (Tokyo), the foreign exchange department (Tokyo) and offices in Marunouchi (Tokyo), Nihonbashi (Tokyo), Otaru (Hokkaido), Yokohama, Nagoya, Kyoto, Osaka, Dojima (Osaka), Osaka-Nishi (Osaka), Kawaguchi (Osaka), Kobe, Hiroshima, Shimonoseki, Moji, Fukuoka, Wakamatsu (Fukuoka), Nagasaki, Shanghai, Bombay, London and New York.[33]

Targeting major corporations

Mitsui Bank went part way towards transforming itself from a bank for the Mitsui family into a bank for major corporations in the 1920s with the first public sale of its shares.

The amount of idle money that commercial banks had on hand began to grow during the recession of 1920 and rapidly increased towards the end of the 1920s. Needless to say, Mitsui Bank was no exception in this respect,[34] and the problem of monetary surplus was exacerbated by the fact that the bank did not relax its restrictive lending policy to any great extent.

At the end of April 1920 the loans extended to Mitsui and Company, Mitsui Mining and Mitsui Gomei amounted to about 94 million yen, or about 26 per cent of the total credit granted by the bank at that time. Of the 94 million yen, that granted to Mitsui and Company is estimated at over 70 million yen and that to Mitsui Gomei at 20 million yen or so, while that to Mitsui Mining was fairly negligible. The total loans held by these three companies fell by about 40 million yen just one year later.[35] Mitsui and Company's sudden repayment of its debt was responsible for this rapid fall as it had been decided that every six months Mitsui Gomei would pay back one million of the 20 million yen it had borrowed from the bank as a subscription for Mitsui Mining. Thus the amount of cash reserves at the bank's head office rose and its idle money surged after August 1920. Part of the idle money was treated as unbudgeted funds available to the bank's major borrowers, in addition to the budgeted funds already available to them.[36]

The major private banks, including Mitsui, made a joint effort to provide relief loans to various industries during the recession. Mitsui Bank played a crucial part in the provision of relief loans to sugar refining companies. These were the first relief loans extended by the bank, in cooperation with Mitsui and Company, which led an initiative to persuade the government, the Bank of Japan and major commercial banks to help the sugar refining industry. Mitsui and Company had an interest in the industry as it had signed an exclusive agency contract with Taiwan Sugar Refining, an affiliate of Mitsui. It was clear that Mitsui and Company remained eager to introduce major borrowers to Mitsui Bank after the bank's reconstruction. Mitsui Bank's share of the total relief loans that major commercial banks provided to sugar refining companies and sugar dealers was about 53 per cent, exceeding even that of the Bank of Taiwan.[37]

The bank first began to extend loans to electric power companies back in 1905, but during and just after the recession of 1920 it drastically increased the amount of such loans. These loans were so large that the total amount lent by the bank exceeded that lent by other banks, and was directly connected to utilization of the bank's huge amount of idle money.[38]

After the establishment of the foreign department at the head office, in 1916 the bank stationed representatives in New York and London and established a branch in Shanghai, its first overseas branch. That was followed by the establishment of a New York agency in 1922, London and Bombay branches in 1924 and a Surabaya office in 1925.[39]

In those days the bank's principal foreign exchange transactions involved the establishment of overdraft contracts with major European and American banks to settle import bills for cotton, and it cleared its debts to the foreign banks with the money it gained by purchasing export bills for raw silk – it purchased about 50 million yen of export bills per annum in the early 1920s.[40] The expansion of its foreign exchange transactions began in 1925, when the amount allocated to such transactions increased from 39.6 million yen to 78.5 million yen.[41] As shown in Table 1.1, the profit margin on the bank's foreign exchange transactions was higher than that on its domestic lending in the mid 1920s.

The bank was also keen to foster a securities business, so in 1926 it established a securities department at its head office – securities-related business had previously been handled by the accounting department.[42] The bank underwrote a huge volume of corporate bonds for electric power companies and railway companies, to most of which it also provided large loans. It was especially eager to be involved in the flotation of foreign currency bonds, with which Japan's five largest electric power companies had found success in the British and US financial markets.

Table 1.1 Profit margin on Mitsui Bank's foreign exchange transactions, 1924–26 (thousand yen)

Branch	1924, 2nd half		1925, 1st half		1925, 2nd half		1926, 1st half		1926, 2nd half	
	Profit or loss (A)	Average yen used (B)	(A)	(B)	(A)	(B)	(A)	(B)	(A)	(B)
Foreign department	861 (20.0)	8533	838 (8.4)	19 923	−363	8277	473 (6.8)	13 944	557 (6.7)	16 442
Shanghai	706 (39.0)	3598	753 (15.7)	9707	531 (9.2)	11 540	521 (9.7)	10 811	341 (9.4)	7197
Surabaya	–	–	–	–	−34	48	−11	401	38 (7.4)	1031
Bombay	−80	186	137 (11.2)	2446	203 (5.5)	7402	295 (5.6)	10 701	98 (4.2)	4641
London	−3	230	17 (4.9)	707	25 (7.0)	701	−23	938	16 (4.0)	776
New York	158 (9.1)	3438	154 (9.5)	3266	40 (5.0)	1 628	103 (4.6)	4553	61 (5.1)	2406
Subtotal (a)	1642 (21.0)	15 614	1864 (10.3)	36 050	402 (2.7)	29 595	1358 (6.6)	41 348	1111 (6.8)	32 494
Yokohama	222 (7.1)	6221	106 (5.1)	4124	274 (6.0)	9062	192 (7.6)	5071	44 (8.2)	4226
Osaka	77 (12.0)	1282	71 (8.7)	1625	56 (12.4)	895	64 (8.1)	1599	49 (27.3)	1418
Kobe	152 (9.8)	3088	46 (2.6)	3472	250 (5.6)	8878	209 (6.4)	6622	32 (4.7)	5372
Subtotal (b)	452 (8.5)	10 592	223 (4.8)	9221	579 (6.2)	18 835	464 (7.0)	13 292	124 (9.0)	11 015
Total (a+b)	2093 (16.0)	26 206	2087 (9.2)	45 271	982 (4.1)	48 430	1823 (6.7)	54 640	1235 (7.0)	35 248

Note: The figures in brackets are the annual profit margins (%). Annual profit margin=profit×2×100/average yen used.

Source: Mitsui Bank, Semi-Annual Reports to the Mitsui Gomei (Sakura Bank archives, unpublished).

It was the Daido Electric Power Company's bonds – issued in 1924 and valued at US$15 million – that the bank first targeted to foster its foreign exchange business. As one of the remittance banks acting for the company, the bank remitted the proceeds from the sale from the US to Japan. Table 1.2 shows that Japan's five largest electric power companies all sold foreign currency bonds from the mid 1920s onwards, and that Daido Electric was the forerunner in this. Mitsui Bank remitted the proceeds of at least three of the eight flotations: twice for Daido Electric and once for Toho Electric.

According to a Daido manager familiar with the 1924 flotation, while Dillon, Read and Company underwrote the bonds, General Electric of the US – one of the largest exporters of electrical equipment to Japan – mediated between Daido and Dillon, Read and Company.[43] Mitsui and Company, which was sole agent for the importation of General Electric products into Japan, was also supposed to play an important role as mediator between the companies concerned in the US and Japan. In the background of this situation was US rivalry with Britain, which was pursuing a 'Buy British' policy through its Trade Facilities Act to stimulate exports.

Mitsui Bank was the trustee for the bonds – valued at US$15 million – that Toho Electric sold in 1925. This was the first occasion on which the bank acted as a trustee for foreign currency bonds issued by the large electric power companies. In a broad sense this was also one of the first steps taken by the bank in its new securities business. The Guaranty Company, a security affiliate of the Guaranty Trust Company, underwrote the bonds.[44] Guaranty Trust made good use of this opportunity to secure a leading role in the underwriting of foreign currency bonds for all five power companies. According to a letter from Raleigh S. Rife of the Guaranty Company to the US Department of State:

> Regarding the Toho Electric Power Co. ... [o]ur friends Lazard Bros. in London have asked us whether we would be interested in an issue of $15,000,000 first mortgage sinking fund 7 per cent gold bonds (exact title not yet determined), to be secured by a first mortgage on all the properties of the company in the Kansai district and in and around Nagoya, Japan. In a sense this is a joint operation between New York and London because they are expecting to float some £300,000 under the trade facilities act,

Table 1.2 Foreign currency bonds sold by Japan's five largest power companies, 1924–26

Date of issue	Company	Amount of issue ($ mil.)	Amount of issue (£10 000)	In Japanese currency	Interest rate (%)	Underwriter	Trustee
1 August 1924	Daido	15.0	–	30 090 000	7.0	Dillon, Read & Co.	IBJ
13 February 1925	Tokyo	–	60	5 857 800	6.0	The Whitehall Trust	–
15 March 1925	Toho	15.0	–	30 090 000	7.0	Guaranty Co.	Mitsui Bank
15 March 1925	Ujigawa	14.0	–	28 084 000	7.0	Lee, Higginson & Co.	IBJ
1 July 1925	Daido	13.5	–	27 081 000	6.5	Dillon, Read & Co.	IBJ
15 July 1925	Toho	–	30	29 289 000	5.0	Prudential Assurance	Mitsui Trust
1 August 1925	Tokyo	24.0	–	48 144 000	6.0	Guaranty Co.	Guaranty Trust
15 July 1926	Toho	10.0	–	20 060 000	6.0	Guaranty Co.	Guaranty Trust

Source: Industrial Bank of Japan (ed.), *Shasai Ichiran* (List of Corporate Bonds) (Tokyo: Industrial Bank of Japan, 1970).

guaranteed by the British Government and at a much lower rate of interest than we could market the bonds here.

We understand that the proceeds of this loan are to be used in part for funding other short-term loans. We know that the company at various times has purchased considerable equipment from American manufacturers, and that this is its first dollar public financing.[45]

Mitsui Bank continued to step up its loans in the years after the recession of 1920, and many of the country's largest companies were among its major borrowers. Table 1.3 shows that in 1924 the list of major borrowers with a debt of five million yen or more was headed by Mitsui and Company with 38 million yen. Most of this debt stemmed from the company's foreign exchange transactions with the bank. Among the other major borrowers were five prominent trading companies and two electric power companies.

Thus the bank succeeded in establishing three main areas to use its excess funds – its lending business, its foreign exchange business

Table 1.3   Mitsui Bank's major borrowers, end of 1924 (yen)

	Domestic transactions	Foreign exchange transactions	Total
Mitsui and Company	230 645	37 465 064	37 695 709
Toyo Menka	55 385	29 881 630	29 937 015
Nihon Menka	2 481 689	5 486 488	7 968 177
Tokyo Electric Light	34 165 373	–	34 165 373
Toho Electric Power	14 500 000	–	14 500 000
Suzuki and Company	14 165 705	–	14 165 705
Mitsui Gomei	11 000 000	–	11 000 000
Oji Paper	9 791 480	–	9 791 480
Ensuiko Sugar	9 789 561	–	9 789 561
Takata and Company	7 329 393	1 366 059	8 695 452
Muslin Spinning and Weaving	7 964 151	–	7 964 151
Fusanosuke Kuhara	7 000 000	–	7 000 000
Nihon Seifun	5 833 278	–	5 833 278
Mitsui Mining	5 269 362	–	5 269 362

Source: Mitsui Bank, 'Special Edition of Research Division's Weekly Report (10 June 1925)', in *The Collected Research Division's Weekly Reports* (Sakura Bank archives, unpublished).

and its securities business – while simultaneously acting as an inter-
mediary for its best customers, especially trading companies and electric power companies, on the British and American financial markets.

The financial panic of 1927

Some of Mitsui's leaders thought that the bank was being damaged by
the Mitsui family (or the Mitsui Gomei) forcing it to pursue a conservative lending policy and sometimes asking it, directly or indirectly, to
provide specific customers with loans. This unsuitable family influence
was likely to prevent the bank from properly screening loan applications. Hence there was no doubt that the Mitsui family's control over
the bank was again causing trouble towards the end of the 1920s.

Mitsui Bank's policy of targeting major corporations as customers
also caused serious difficulties during and after the financial panic of
1927. Although the bank had tried to avoid bad debts by carefully
selecting its loan clientele, ironically this caused the bank even
more serious problems. The bank fell into trouble as a result its
loans to Suzuki and Company (Suzuki Shoten – after its bankruptcy
in 1927 its business was taken over by one of predecessors of the
present Nissho Iwai Corporation), a large Japanese trading company,
and its loans to Tokyo Electric Light.

The bank's loans to Suzuki rose to 60–70 million yen just before
Suzuki went bankrupt in the spring of 1927. These loans can be
divided into three categories: loans to Suzuki itself, which amounted
to about 14 million yen;[46] loans to Suzuki's four affiliates, which
totalled about 21 million yen;[47] and call loans of 39 million yen to
the Bank of Taiwan, which had an extremely close relationship with
Suzuki.[48] The loans were so large that the bank was in danger of
falling victim to a chain-reaction bankruptcy along with Suzuki and
the Bank of Taiwan. Unfortunately the bank's course of action made
matters worse, that is, it stuck strictly to its restrictive lending policy
in order to protect own interests rather than attending to the public
role it should have played as Japan's largest commercial bank. The
bank's decision to call in its loans to the Bank of Taiwan and Suzuki
was acted on so quickly that it was accused of triggering both their
bankruptcy and the 1927 panic.

In March 1927 the failure of Tokyo Watanabe Bank was reported
in the newspapers while a debate was still in progress in the Diet

about the abolition of the 'Earthquake Bill' and the possibility of providing special government aid to seriously affected banks. This caused people to feel jittery about the safety of their money and a run on the banks developed. A state of panic was reached in April, when even the top banks were forced temporarily to suspend their business and the government was obliged to promulgate a three-week moratorium to calm the situation. During the panic the minister of finance, Korekiyo Takahashi (a well-known public financier, later assassinated by a young right-wing army officer on 26 February 1936) provided the Bank of Japan with 500 million yen of state funds and the Bank of Taiwan with 200 million yen to limit the damage and help restore order to the financial system.

The panic and the consequent enactment of the Bank Law to protect depositors resulted in the banking industry undergoing considerable consolidation. Thereafter Mitsui Bank's deposits began to swell. Its total deposits amounted to 560 million yen by the end of 1927, an increase of over 100 million yen in one year, reflecting the trend towards the concentration of deposits among the five largest banks (Mitsui, Mitsubishi, Dai-Ichi, Sumitomo and Yasuda) (Table 1.4).[49] As a result Mitsui Bank became even more concerned about utilizing its excess funds and decided mainly to inject them into its foreign exchange and securities business. The bank had particular success in underwriting public and corporate bonds, conducting trust business related to electric power companies' foreign currency bonds and buying and selling domestic and foreign short-term securities. Between the end of 1926 and the end of 1928 the bank's total security holdings increased by about 110 million yen, broken down into 93 million yen, 1.2 million pounds sterling and 4.7 million dollars.[50]

First of all the bank invested about 20 million yen in British and American government bonds (valued at 1.19 million pounds sterling and at 4.7 million dollars), using them as collateral for overdrafts from major British and American banks in 1927. The bank's particular aim was to improve its creditworthyness in the international financial market by establishing a closer relationship with large British banks such as Barclays. In those days the bank's management used to call this the 'self-sufficiency of exchange fund principle'.[51]

Second, it was quite natural for the bank to focus on expanding its purchase of export bills and the settlement of import bills, especially with Mitsui and Company and Toyo Menka, an affiliate of the

Table 1.4 Japan's five largest commercial banks, increase in deposits, 1923–30 (thousand yen)

Year end	Mitsui	Mitsubishi		Sumitomo		Dai-Ichi		Yasuda	
	Amount	Amount	(%)*	Amount	(%)*	Amount	(%)*	Amount	(%)*
1923 (A)	417 548	307 326	74	344 059	82	344 435	82	568 817	135
1924	408 583	303 004	74	376 589	92	346 473	85	572 514	140
1925	439 999	311 826	71	415 909	95	366 349	83	571 728	130
1926	455 844	328 833	72	435 149	95	390 821	86	622 504	137
1927	560 334	470 586	84	552 780	99	520 884	93	713 275	127
1928	605 609	562 252	93	642 862	106	597 301	99	721 945	119
1929	660 373	599 701	91	662 680	100	628 730	95	658 094	100
End June 1930	648 873	593 393	91	670 861	103	634 394	98	636 885	98
Amount of increase (B)	231 325	286 067		326 802		289 959		72 068	
B/A (%)	55	93		95		84		13	

*Percentage comparison with Mitsui Bank's deposits.

Source: Mitsui Bank, 'Special Edition of Research Division's Weekly Report (17 February 1931)', in The Collected Research Division's Weekly Reports (Sakura Bank archives, unpublished).

company. Table 1.5 shows the company's exchange transactions with eight major domestic and foreign banks headed by Yokohama Specie Bank.

Although the huge amount of idle money the bank had was the most important factor in the rapid increase in securities investment and bond underwriting, it was not the only reason for these activities. Another factor was its bad debt problem. The bank considered that the securities business, especially the underwriting of corporate bonds, would be effective in solving this problem. Hence it underwrote corporate bonds for some debtor customers so that they could pay off their debts with the proceeds from the flotation of these bonds.

For example Tokyo Electric Light's debt to the bank had soared after 1926, and by the end of March 1928 had reached 85.8 million yen, or about 21 per cent of the bank's total outstanding loans, excluding call loan. Nineteen million yen of Tokyo Electric's debt was repaid from the proceeds of the flotation of the company's domestic bonds in May 1928, and in June 1928 49.3 million yen was repaid from the proceeds of two sales of the company's foreign currency bonds, valued respectively at £4.5 million and $70 million. As a result the company reduced its debt to the bank to zero.[52] How eager the large banks, including Mitsui Bank, were to retrieve their loans to electric power companies by means of foreign currency bond flotation is illustrated by the sale of Toho Electric Power bonds and Tokyo Electric Light bonds, underwritten by the Guaranty Company. The proceeds of these bonds were to be used to fund other short-term loans (in the case of the first sale of Toho Electric Power bonds in 1925), 'to pay the corporation's existing indebtedness' (in the case of the second sale of Toho Electric Power bonds in 1926), 'for the payment of all existing bank loans' (in the case of the third sale Toho Electric Power bonds in 1929), 'to pay off the company's existing bank indebtedness' (in the case of the sale of Tokyo Electric Light bonds in 1925) and 'for the retirement of all outstanding bank loans' (in the case of the second sale Tokyo Electric Light bonds in 1928).[53]

Between the end of March 1927 and the end of 1929 the bank's deposits increased by a further 170 million yen. Funds for domestic lending were fixed at around 400 million yen during the period, so the majority of the increase in deposits was again put into its

Table 1.5 Mitsui and Company's exchange transactions with banks, 1926–29 (10 thousand yen)

	Mitsui	Yokohama Specie Bank	Taiwan	Chosen	Sumitomo	Hong Kong and Shanghai	Chartered	International	Other	House bills	Total
1st half 1926	5731	8647	3476	844	171	1928	1997	1493	3478	5803	33 568
% of total	17.1	25.8	10.4	2.5	0.5	5.7	5.9	4.4	10.4	17.3	100.0
2nd half 1926	6271	6089	1960	1397	139	2931	813	1774	3000	4432	28 806
% of total	21.8	21.1	6.8	4.8	0.5	10.2	2.8	6.2	10.4	15.4	100.0
1st half 1927	4981	6727	1533	1695	190	1921	1340	2128	2941	5855	29 311
% of total	17.0	23.0	5.2	5.8	0.6	6.6	4.6	7.3	10.0	20.0	100.0
2nd half 1927	5331	9421	434	606	143	2306	1237	2648	2518	4504	29 148
% of total	18.3	32.3	1.5	2.1	0.5	7.9	4.2	9.1	8.6	15.6	100.0
1st half 1928	7335	7787	258	635	1264	1791	1097	1734	3619	6144	31 664
% of total	23.2	24.6	0.8	2.0	4.0	5.7	3.5	5.5	11.4	19.9	100.0
2nd half 1928	7469	6554	183	94	1287	1461	1055	2071	2341	5600	28 115
% of total	26.6	23.3	0.7	0.3	4.6	5.2	3.8	7.4	8.3	19.9	100.0
1st half 1929	7231	8202	449	1043	797	1510	1565	1784	3759	7671	34 011
% of total	21.3	24.1	1.3	3.1	2.3	4.4	4.6	5.2	11.1	22.6	100.0
2nd half 1929	4566	10943	776	721	1522	2276	1896	1241	2534	7027	33 502
% of total	13.6	31.8	2.3	2.3	4.5	6.8	5.7	3.7	7.6	21.0	100.0

Source: Mitsui and Company, Semi-Annual Reports from Mitsui Bunko (Mitsui Research Institute for Social and Economic History archives, unpublished).

Table 1.6 Mitsui Bank's credit to Mitsui and Company and its affiliates, 1928–30 (yen)

	Mitsui and Company		Toyo Menka		Southern Cotton		Total	
	End March 1928	End December 1930	End March 1928	End December 1930	End March 1928	End December 1930	End March 1928	End December 1930
Bills discounted	4 021 933	2 380 167	7 997 735	–	–	–	12 019 668	2 380 167
Loans on bills	1 819 654	10 561 570	5 698 002	40 000	–	–	7 517 656	10 601 570
Overdrafts	2 657 090	1 846 054	10 241 425	1 057 391	–	434 629	12 898 515	2 903 445
Foreign exchange purchased	36 054 011	29 709 476	13 568 755	7 560 062	2 500 588	6 635 538	52 123 356	43 905 077
Interest bills	10 893 263	349 315	556 624	1 561 287	7 177 809	–	18 627 697	1 910 603
Other	11 221 075	303 485	–	–	–	–	11 221 075	303 485
Guarantees and endorsements	306 048	–	–	–	–	–	306 048	–
Total credit	66 973 076	45 150 071	38 062 544	10 218 741	9 678 398	7 070 168	114 714 018	62 438 980
Acceptance	13 909 579	138 575	1 270 415	1 459 897	–	–	–	–
Deposits at Mitsui Bank	2 155 394[1] 450 000[2] 42 895 851[3]	2 672 205[1] 1 000 834[2] 31 932 314[3]	661 144[1] 750 000[4]	273 257[1] 700 000[4]	–	–	–	–

Notes: 1. Current deposits. 2. Special current deposits. 3. Time deposits. 4. Notice deposits.

Source: Mitsui Bank, *Documents on the Bank's Substantial Credit to Customers* (Sakura Bank archives, unpublished).

securities and foreign exchange business, while the rest was added to its reserves. As these reserves swelled, the bank's outlook changed considerably. The reserves had reached more than 70 million yen by the end of May 1927, and the proportion deposited in non-interest-bearing current accounts at the Bank of Japan had risen to more than 60 million yen. Until the panic of 1927 the bank had provided a considerable number of call loans to government financial institutions such as the Bank of Taiwan and thus turned its idle money into working funds.[54]

While the ranking of the eight major banks had not been fixed, no doubt some kind of order had been established before the Bank of Taiwan ran into financial difficulties. In the early 1920s Mitsui Bank had ranked third or fourth, with the Yokohama Specie Bank and the Bank of Taiwan at the top. After 1926, however, the bank had expanded its foreign exchange transactions with Mitsui and Company, as though sweeping up the Bank of Taiwan's transactions, and was at last able to assume a leading position, ranking alongside Yokohama Specie Bank in respect of foreign exchange transactions with Mitsui and Company after 1928. As shown in Table 1.6, the bank's various financial transactions with the company and its affiliates at the end of the 1920s amounted to more than 100 million yen, reflecting the expansion of the bank's foreign exchange transactions with these companies.

Summary

Mitsui Bank was established in 1876 and until the early 1900s acted as the nucleus of the businesses run by the Mitsui family. In the 1890s the bank adopted a policy of gaining control of companies by providing them with loans and then taking them into the Mitsui group. This policy was eventually abandoned when the bank was nearly forced into suspending payments during the recession of 1900–1. It was Takashi Masuda who succeeded in rebuilding the bank, based on sound commercial banking principles. In 1902 he introduced a new lending policy whereby borrowing companies would be kept at arm's length rather than drawn into the fold.

The bank was forced yet again to reform its lending policy before and after World War I. It took positive steps to increase the amount of deposits and loans, and devoted considerable energy to establishing an efficient branch network and head office. In the 1920s it established three main target areas for the use of its funds: its lending business, its foreign exchange business and its securities business.

The bank did not act as the main bank of the Mitsui-affiliated companies because control by the Mitsui family meant that it could not use its own discretion as lender of last resort. Furthermore Mitsui and Company did not need huge loans from the bank except during the depressed economic period before World War I. The company originally relied on Yokohama Specie Bank for its foreign exchange transactions, but in 1926, as Mitsui Bank's surplus funds grew ever larger, the company increased its foreign exchange transactions with the bank and the latter assumed the leading position in such transactions in 1928.

2
Towards a Closer Relationship with Industry, 1930–43

During the 1920s most of Japan's zaibatsu-affiliated banks tried to turn themselves into public companies by reorganizing themselves into joint-stock companies, offering shares to the public, appointing salaried managers to top management, and calling in outside directors and auditors. Nonetheless, at the beginning of the 1930s they were still essentially under the control of the zaibatsu families and as a result did not feel overly responsible for bailing out major Japanese industries on the verge of collapse.

Banking before and during World War II

During the 1930s and the first half of the 1940s, a period characterized by economic depression and world-wide warfare, Japan's major banks not only had to address their own troubles but were also asked to meet various demands by major industries and the government, such as financial support for the reorganization of industry and industrial mobilization for war.

Governmental authorities such as the Ministry of Finance and the Bank of Japan interfered in private banks' affairs and fund control as a controlled economy developed in Japan. It is interesting to note that the Ministry of Commerce and Industry also aggressively interfered in private banks' affairs. The ministry considered the banks' loan policies to be excessively conservative and self-seeking, and wanted them to increase their loans to the heavy and chemical industries. This should not be interpreted as interference by the military, although the ministry often cooperated with the latter. Rather it was because the ministry had failed to rehabilitate Japan's major industries through large-scale mergers and had become aware that it would not be able to poster these industries without the support of the zaibatsu-affiliated banks. During the same period Japan's financial authorities, led by the Ministry of Finance, gradually increased their interference in order to make the banking system stronger.

The interference in private banks' affairs by authorities concerned with industry was specific to Japan after the Great Depression, and later the repetition of such interference helped the Ministry of International Trade and Industry to develop a strong industrial policy that was also specific to Japan.

Here we shall examine the relationship between the government and the banks, as outlined by Takafusa Nakamura (1998) and in an official history of Fuji Bank.

In January 1930, having lifted the embargo on gold in September 1917, Japan returned to the gold standard at the old parity in an attempt to stabilize the economy. However the worldwide panic resulting from the US stock market crash of 1929 had already begun to affect Japan, and the combination of world depression and the government's deflationary policy thrust the Japanese economy into deep recession. Between 1929 and 1931 the wholesale price index dropped more than 30 per cent, share prices fell about 30 per cent and silk prices on the Yokohama exchange halved. The government had to resort to deficit financing both to fight the recession and to meet increased military expenditure as a result of the events in Manchuria in 1931–32. Government bonds were issued, and in December 1931 the embargo on gold was reimposed.

Low interest rates and the decline of the yen against the major overseas currencies because of the reimposed embargo on gold were important factors in the recovery of the economy – the depreciation of the yen led to a flood of exports, and the Ministry of Finance's policy of keeping down interest rates gave businesses the opportunity to finance major expansion projects relatively cheaply. After 1936 the production of military matériel was increased to support the war with China. The Ministry of Finance and the Ministry of Commerce and Industry then set about controlling all aspects of the economy because Japan's international balance of payments was under pressure from rising imports, and the surge in military spending combined with the growing domestic demand had aroused fears of inflation.

In September 1937, just after the outbreak of war with China, the first of three epoch-making laws was passed. The Law for the Extraordinary Adjustment of Funds (*Rinji Shikin Chosei Ho*) enabled the government to examine the long-term financial needs of enterprises and regulate their procurement of long-term funds. The intention was to classify industries into categories according to their national importance and to channel limited resources into the military-supply sector, and on a case-by-case basis into less important sectors. No doubt this law substantially influenced the long-term lending activities of private banks.

In 1940 the government issued the Order Concerning the Operation of Funds by Banks (*Ginko tou Shikin Unyo Rei*) to place the supply of short-term loans by financial institutions under its control. And in 1942 the Bank of Japan Law was amended to allow the central bank to govern financial policy and ensure the necessary supply of money, under the direction of the minister of finance. In the same year the War Finance Bank (Senji Kinyu Kinko) was established to fund extra munitions production; it also provided loans to companies that were having difficulty raising funds through normal banking channels.

In this wartime situation the government attempted to consolidate the economy through the merger or reorganization of banks and major industries. For example it urged banks to merge not only in order to protect depositors and creditors but also so that they could play a more direct role in the purchase of government bonds and in supporting the policy of low interest rates. As a result of such mergers the number of commercial banks fell from 1031 at the end of 1928 (the year the Bank Law went into effect) to 346 at the end of 1938, 186 at the end of 1941 (when the Pacific War began) and 61 at the end of 1945.

In November 1943 the Ministry of Munitions (Gunjusho) was established, taking over the functions of the Planning Board (Kikakuin) and most of the functions of the Ministry of Commerce and Industry, which were abolished. The primary objective of the Ministry of Munitions was to increase the production of aeroplanes. Companies identified as vitally important to the war effort were designated as 'munitions industries', and their presidents were given the status of public officials with responsibility for meeting production targets. They were given the authority to override any decisions made by their shareholders when carrying out the orders of government ministers.

Along with the establishment of the Ministry of Munitions, the government introduced a new law that obliged certain financial institutions to provide loans to designated munitions companies. This meant that the ministry, as a successor to the Ministry of Commerce and Industry, was able to direct major banks to administer loans towards the end of the Pacific War.[1]

Until the Showa depression, Mitsui Bank was notable for being the largest, oldest and most influential zaibatsu-affiliated bank. After the depression it was notable for assuming responsibility for the banking affairs of major industries in all sectors of the economy, not merely of Mitsui businesses. In fact the bank was the only large bank capable of separating itself almost completely from the control of the zaibatsu family before the dissolution of the zaibatsu after World War II. Twice during the depression it accumulated bad debts and faced uncertainty about its creditworthiness, and in time the Mitsui family came to lose interest in managing a commercial bank – a misfortune the bank was able to turn into a blessing.

Mitsui Bank's change of lending policy

Despite the problems experienced by Mitsui Bank in the late 1920s in respect of bad debts, such as those incurred by Suzuki and Company and Tokyo Electric Light, it managed to weather its troubles without changing its conservative lending policy. The bank was able to redeem its loans to the Bank of Taiwan and Suzuki very quickly, and as discussed in the previous chapter, Tokyo Electric Light paid off its debt with the proceeds of corporate bonds underwritten by the bank.

However during and after the Showa depression, starting in 1930, the bank's bad debt problem became more serious than at any time since its reorganization into a joint stock company in 1909. (In this case bad debts meant the totality of non-interest-bearing loans, uncollectable loans and the like.) Not only were the debts huge, but also a lot of the loans were in conflict with the bank's sound lending policy, and therefore some of the bank's managing directors, general managers and branch managers advocated the complete reversal of the policy. As the deteriorating economic circumstances were also badly affecting its foreign exchange business, the bank felt impelled to change its lending policy drastically.

Table 2.1 shows that the total number and amount of bad debts increased in the second half of 1932, even though the depression bottomed out in 1931. The figures in the first three columns include loans the bank had trouble collecting and pre-existing bad debts. The table does not include the huge amount owed by Tokyo Electric Light between 1932 and 1934. If this is added, at the end of 1932 the total amount of bad debts reached 110 million yen, or a quarter of the bank's total outstanding loans.

Here we shall examine precisely how and why the bank's loans to Tokyo Electric Light turned into a bad debt. In the late 1920s the company was pushed into a policy of free-spending by its managing directors, who were the major shareholders and represented the Koshu group (a group of investors from the Yamanashi prefecture, west of Tokyo. Koshu was the previous name of the prefecture). When the three major banks failed to stop executive vice-president Shohachi Wakao's promotion to president, Mitsubishi and Yasuda Banks discontinued all transactions with the company. Only Mitsui Bank remained, and it provided the company with relief loans. Thereafter the bank prioritized the company's reform, sending three business leaders to the company's board of directors.[2]

One of the main reasons for the bank daring to deviate from its lending policy was that Takuma Dan had demanded such action from the bank, fearing that the bankruptcy of Tokyo Electric Light would have a bad effect on Mitsui and Company and Mitsui Mining. (Dan, a graduate of the Massachusetts Institute of Technology, was assassinated by a young right in 1932 had assumed the presidency of Mitsui Gomei in 1914.) The bank put up little resistance to the company's request because of the long-standing relationship between the two.[3]

Although a substantial proportion of the relief loans extended in 1927 was repaid to the bank, Tokyo Electric Light's debt to the bank soared rapidly again in the second half of 1929, when the company failed in its bid to raise funds by selling foreign currency bonds. In April 1930 the group of British and US banks underwriting the bonds began to press the company to reform itself more drastically.[4] On behalf of the syndicate Burnett Walker, vice-president of the Guaranty Trust Company and its security affiliate, the Guaranty

Table 2.1 Mitsui Bank, bad debts, 1931–36 (thousands of yen)

	Questionable loans			Bad debts			Amount written down	
	Number	Total amount	% of total outstanding loans	Number	Total amount	% of total outstanding loans	Number	Total amount
1st half 1931	50	45 000	10.9	–	–	–	2	501
2nd half 1931	44	47 000	10.8	2	9420	2.2	19	3909
1st half 1932	49	48 000	10.9	2	9160	2.1		
2nd half 1932	54	53 000	12.3	4	16 880	4.0	7	3573
1st half 1933	50	45 000	11.6	4	14 000	3.6		
2nd half 1933	41	39 000	9.5	4	12 840	3.2	4	1533
1st half 1934	37	35 000	9.5	6	11 750	3.2		
2nd half 1934	35	31 000	8.1	4	11 000	3.0	4	986
1st half 1935	33	30 000	7.9	6	10 500	2.8		
2nd half 1935	31	28 000	6.2	3	9640	2.2	3	103.9
1st half 1936	27	26 000	5.9	2	1730	0.4		

Source: The Secret Story and Documents on Mitsui Bank (Sakura Bank archives, unpublished).

Company, travelled to Japan to demand the dismissal of Tokyo Electric's president, Wakao, and reduction of the dividend rate from 6 per cent to zero. When the company failed to comply with his requests, Walker asked the government to intervene. The government was vulnerable in that it would have to convert its 5 per cent sterling bonds, valued at £23.44 million and due in January 1931, with the help of the group of British and US underwriters and would therefore be badly affected by the company's financial difficulties.[5]

The key men in the affair were Thomas Lamont, a partner in J. P. Morgan and Company who was staying in London as representative of the British and US syndicate that was underwriting loans extended by the German government, and Minister of Finance Inoue, who was responsible for conversion of the bonds. After a series of negotiations, on 9 May a memorandum partly accepting Walker's requests was handed over to him, and a contract for conversion of the Japanese government bonds was signed by the representatives on the same day.[6] In short Walker succeeded in realizing much of what he sought.

According to the memorandum, the reduction of the dividend rate to 5 per cent and the lowering of Wakao's rank from president to vice-president of Tokyo Electric would be duly carried out. But at a share-holders' meeting in June 1930, many large shareholders unexpectedly rose in protest against the management and eventually all the managing directors and directors representing the Koshu group – headed by the president, Wakao – were forced to resign.[7] As the three directors sent by Mitsui Bank to the company remained as leading members of its board of directors, the bank was forced to become involved in the company's management and to place the company under the bank's supervision on behalf of the British and US underwriting syndicate.

Internal and external debate on the bank's lending policy escalated in the second half of 1929, when the government decided to return to the gold standard. One member of the management team proposed a reform plan under which the bank would be set free from the Mitsui family's control, enabling a closer relationship to be built between the bank and industry.[8] However Mitsui and Company, which still wielded considerable influence over the bank's lending policy, insisted that all Mitsui enterprises should unite themselves under the Mitsui family's control and that the bank should take greater responsibility for their banking affairs.[9]

Outside the bank, the government too was opposed to the lending policies of the large commercial banks. In particular the Ministry of Commerce and Industry was eager for the zaibatsu-affiliated banks to relax their policies and to work closely with industry in the reorganization and rationalization of its operations.

As the ministry's industrial rationalization policy was the prototype for the industrial policy of the Ministry of International Trade and Industry the two had many features in common. The industrial rationalization policy, introduced at the end of the 1920s and based on the US and German models was aimed at promoting productivity by introducing more efficient machines into factories, improving the efficiency of business operations, cutting production costs and so on. One of the most remarkable features of the policy, compared with its foreign counterparts, was that it aimed to cut excess capacity and workers on a large scale by means of corporate mergers.[10] This was to confront the problem of excessive competition among companies that were too small and weak to compete with foreign companies.

Most loans extended by the large private banks (at the ministry's request) to make the merger project successful were relief loans. For Mitsui Bank, however, such loans contravened its lending policy. The government's difficulty in obtaining assistance from the large private banks and in pursuing the merger project provided a reason for establishing government control of the banks' funds and for ranking industries according to their priority for loans, as noted above.

The banks' executives took strong precautions against the expected tightening of their cash position. That is why Mitsui Bank did not relax its lending policy and refused to adhere to the government's requests. Also behind Mitsui Bank's precautions was the considerable pressure it was experiencing as a result of its loans to electric power companies, given that the British and US underwriting syndicate was turning its back on these companies.[11]

In 1931 the bank stepped up its foreign exchange and securities business in order to use its growing excess funds more profitably. Between the end of 1930 and June 1931 there had been an increase of 35 million yen in the bank's average deposit balance and a decrease of 33 million yen in its average balance for domestic loans. As a result, about 68 million yen emerged as new funds to be utilized.

Most of the funds were put into domestic and foreign short-term securities – such as Japanese Treasury Bills, rice certificates, Japanese Treasury Bonds, Indian Government Sterling Bonds, Exchequer Bills and Indian Treasury Bills – or deposited as foreign currency deposits at five big commercial banks and a merchant bank in Britain. As can be seen from Table 2.2, the bank bought Indian Treasury Bills valued at 20.3 million rupees and sold or retired 12.25 million rupees' worth during the first half of 1931, leaving a balance of Indian Treasury Bills valued at 11.05 million rupees at the end of June 1931. The bank also bought Exchequer Bills valued at £1.05 million during the first half of 1931, but did not sell or retire any of these. The bank's deposits at British financial institutions at the end of June 1931 amounted to £1650 thousand: £500 thousand at the Midland Bank, £400 thousand at Barclays, £300 thousand at Rothschilds, £250 thousand at Lloyds and £200 thousand at National Provincial.[12]

In the second half of 1931 the bank became even more enthusiastic about purchasing British Exchequer Bills to increase the short-term utilization of otherwise idle funds. For most of these purchases the bank used pounds sterling obtained in exchange for dollars secured in the purchase of export bills destined for the US. The bank bought British Exchequer Bills valued at £7.92 million during the second half of 1931, about 7.5 times the amount purchased during the first half of the year. Besides British Exchequer Bills, the bank purchased additional Indian Treasury Bills and Indian Government Sterling Bonds.[13]

To increase its returns from the investment by avoiding the exchange risks involved in the purchase of British Exchequer Bills, the bank made forward sales exchange contracts amounting to $16 330 000 instead of the equivalent amount in pounds sterling when it purchased the bills. Two mistakes were made in this transaction: one was the currency chosen and the other was that the forward sales exchange contracts were not sufficient to cover the purchase of the Exchequer Bills.

Unfortunately, when Britain withdrew from the gold standard on 21 September 1931 the pound sterling quickly weakened. Crucially the bank had had an overbought position of £8 541 000 and an oversold position of $16 334 000 on 19 September 1931. It was the sum, rather than the difference, of these that was left exposed to the known exchange risk then. To remedy its oversold position it

Table 2.2 Short-term securities bought by Mitsui Bank, 1st half of 1931

	Securities bought and deposits			Balance at term end	
	Amount	Book value (yen)	Profit margin	Amount	Book value (yen)
Japanese Treasury Bills (yen)	83 870 000	83 648 461	2.19	35 450 000	35 363 523
Rice Certificates (yen)	11 842 886	11 808 526	3.48	–	–
5% Japanese Treasury Bonds (yen)	3 550 000	3 545 800	5.02	3 550 000	3 545 800
5.5% Indian Government Sterling Bonds (£)	500 000	4 771 433	6.14	500 000	4 664 615
6% Indian Government Sterling Bonds (£)	500 000	4 894 030	6.21	500 000	4 894 030
Indian Treasury Bills (rupees)	20 300 000	14 763 636	4.21	11 050 000	7 888 201
Exchequer Bills (£)	1 050 000	10 280 992	2.45	1 050 000	10 280 992
Deposits at foreign financial institutions (£)	2 450 000	24 113 682	2.73	1 650 000*	16 226 612
Total book value		157 826 560			82 863 773

*The £1 650 000 is broken down as follows: £500 000 in Midland Bank, £400 000 in Barclays, £300 000 in Rothschilds, £250 000 in Lloyds, £200 000 in Natwest (previously National Provincial).

Source: Mitsui Bank, Semi-Annual Reports to the Mitsui Gomei (Sakura Bank archives, unpublished), especially the report for the first half of 1931.

promptly purchased $16 million from the Yokohama Specie Bank to enable settlement on 21 September 1931. However its overbought position continued, and its latent exchange losses expanded rapidly in proportion to the pound sterling's depreciation.

The bank's overbought position of £8 541 000 consisted mainly of British Exchequer Bills valued at £4 410 000, Indian Government Sterling Bonds valued at £1 320 000, British Consols valued at £2 760 000 and deposits at British commercial and merchant banks valued at £900 000 (£400 000 at Barclays, £300 000 at the Midland and £200 000 at Rothschilds).[14]

The exchange losses incurred by the bank due to the pound sterling's depreciation of 30 per cent was estimated at about 24 million yen.[15] The bank was being driven into such a corner that it might have to disclose these huge losses in its financial report for the six months ending 31 December 1931. If that happened the bank would face serious doubt about its creditworthiness and there would be runs on the bank. The only solution to the problem would be for Japan to withdraw from the gold standard and for the yen to depreciate.

On 11 December, unable to maintain cabinet unity because of differences of opinion between Home Minister Kenzo Adachi and other cabinet members, Prime Minister Reijiro Wakatsuki and his ministers in the Minseito (Constitutional Democratic Party) administration were obliged to resign *en masse*. Finance Minister Inoue had wanted to maintain the gold standard at all costs. On 13 December, two days after the collapse of the Minseito administration, the Seiyukai (Friend of the Constitutional Government) Party formed a new cabinet. Its finance minister, Takahashi, quickly introduced a gold embargo and put a stop to gold conversion.[16] Owing to the dramatic change of administration, the yen depreciated quickly and the yen–pound exchange rate was almost restored to the level it had stood at before Britain's withdrawal from the gold standard. Thus Mitsui Bank's problem with foreign exchange losses was conveniently resolved.[17]

The yen continued to depreciate in 1932, bringing the bank handsome foreign exchange earnings thanks to its enormous overbought position in pounds sterling, but simultaneously its bad debt problem became more serious. This was because the depreciation of the yen had caused Japan's large electric power companies – including Tokyo Electric Light, which had issued dollar bonds – serious foreign exchange losses.[18] This new problem, coupled with the effects of the domestic depression, drove the power companies into financial difficulty.

Tokyo Electric Light failed in its bid to convert its domestic bonds (worth 40 million yen and maturing at the end of October 1932) because of a shrinkage of the domestic bond market. Of course Mitsui Bank was almost equally to blame. To do nothing would have not only caused financial difficulty for the company but also triggered concern about the bank's creditworthiness. Although the bank asked Tokyo Electric's bond holders to subscribe to the refunding bonds, the total amount subscribed to was only 2 762 000 yen, less than 7 per cent of the value of the bonds to be issued. If the bank had subscribed to the remaining bonds on its own the total credit extended to Tokyo Electric would have reached about 100 million yen (Table 2.3). In short it was clear that the unsold bonds were too much for the bank to subscribe by itself.

Eventually the bank was able to resolve the problem with the help of the Industrial Bank of Japan (IBJ), which subscribed to 14 109 500 yen's worth of bonds (Table 2.4). At the same time, to help the IBJ the executive director of Mitsui Bank, Ikeda, persuaded Mitsui's leaders, who were unsure about whether to accept the IBJ's offer, to agree to Oji Paper (a Mitsui affiliate) acquiring Karafuto Kogyo, to which the IBJ had extended a huge amount of bad loans. The passage of the agreement became easier when Dan (president of Mitsui

Table 2.3 Credit extended by Mitsui Bank to Tokyo Electric Light and its affiliate, October 1932 (yen)

Unsecured loans	45 000 000
Loans to Toden Securities	15 000 000
Loans on Tokyo Electric Light bonds	870 000
Loans on Tokyo Electric Light shares	9 090 000
Subtotal	69 960 000
Unsold bonds	28 000 000
Grand total	97 960 000
The bank's total outstanding loans (approx.)	400 000 000
Paid-in capital	60 000 000
Authorized capital	100 000 000

Source: *The Secret Story of Documents on Mitsui Bank* (Sakura Bank archives, unpublished).

Table 2.4 Allotment of Tokyo Electric Light refunding bonds (yen)

	Title holder	*Allotment*
On day of issue of the bonds	Holders of matured bonds	2 762 000
	Mitsui Bank	37 238 000
On 25 October 1932	Holders of matured bonds	2 762 000
	Mitsui Bank	27 928 500
	IBJ	9 309 500
In November 1932	Holders of matured bonds	2 762 000
	Mitsui Bank	22 928 500
	IBJ	14 309 500

Source: *The Secret Story of Documents on Mitsui Bank* (Sakura Bank archives, unpublished).

Gomei and the most influential opponent of this acquisition) was shot and killed by a young right-wing activist in March 1932. On 18 October 1932 it was announced that the two sides had agreed that the following May three large paper manufacturing companies – Oji Paper, Fuji Paper (an affiliate of Oji Paper) and Karafuto Kogyo – would be consolidated into one company (under the name of Oji Paper) with 150 million yen of authorized capital. Thus the IBJ's bad loans to Karafuto Kogyo were quickly changed into good loans to Oji Paper, newly established in 1933.[19]

The five large electric power companies' financial difficulties lessened in 1933, when their problem with foreign exchange losses receded a little and the demand for electric power began to recover. However they still needed to reduce their fund-raising costs (achieved by converting their outstanding high-interest-bearing bonds into low-interest-bearing ones) to escape fully from their financial difficulties. Major banks and trust companies set up a number of underwriting syndicates to refund the bonds at a lower interest rate. For example in 1934–35 seven banks and two trust companies, headed by Mitsui Bank as a trustee bank, set up such syndicates for Tokyo Electric Light. In this way Mitsui Bank's bad loans to Tokyo Electric Light had also changed into good loans by 1935.[20]

Although the Japanese munitions and export industries had been boosted by the war in Manchuria and by the yen's depreciation after Japan's withdrawal from the gold standard, Mitsui Bank still tended to stick to its policy of extending loans mainly to major companies, especially Mitsui and Company and its affiliates. Foreign exchange business still held great appeal for the bank, though the purchase of foreign bonds and bills was prohibited by such laws as the Foreign Exchange Control Law. This was the main reason why the bank lost its competitive ability to attract deposits – deposits in the bank, touching bottom in March 1932, increased fairly slowly – until 1935, while deposits in other large banks (except Mitsubishi Bank) increased rapidly and continuously (Table 2.5). Table 2.5 also shows that both Mitsui Bank and Mitsubishi Bank were able to reduce their loan balances for a number of years while those of other large banks increased slowly and steadily.

Mitsui Bank put the funds newly available from the increase in deposits and decrease in the loan balance into its foreign exchange and securities businesses. Roughly speaking, the bank put to work 220 million yen in new funds, 160 million yen of which came from the increase in deposits and the rest from the 60 million yen decrease in loans between the end of March 1932 (not shown in Table 2.5) and the end of June 1935. It bought long-term government bonds valued at 180 million yen and expanded its foreign exchange operations by 40 million yen. However radical this use of funds might look, the bank essentially maintained an old-fashioned, extremely conservative and irresponsible attitude towards its banking affairs with industry.[21]

However the bank began to change its policy of lending more or less exclusively to major companies after 1935, when its bad debt problem may have eased but it had become evident that it was inferior to other large banks when it came to attracting deposits and providing loans.[22] The bank established a committee to promote transactions with firms in 1935, followed in 1936 by reform of its foreign exchange operations and abolition of its securities department at head office.[23] These steps were taken in accordance with the bank's decision to discontinue its policy of using its excess funds for its foreign exchange and securities operations.

To promote its business with non-major firms the bank first targeted the Mitsui enterprises, especially Mitsui and Company, Mitsui Mining, Toyo Menka and the Kanegafuchi Spinning Company. Table 2.6 shows that the bank's loans to Kanegafuchi Spinning amounted to about 72 million yen at the end of June 1937, a remarkable increase since 1935. After 1937 a stream of Mitsui enterprises, following in the footsteps of Kanegafuchi Spinning, became the bank's main commercial borrowers.[24]

Table 2.5 Japan's six largest banks' deposits and loans, 1931–37 (million yen)

	Deposits						Loans					
	Mitsui	Mitsubishi	Dai-Ichi	Sumitomo	Yasuda	Sanwa	Mitsui	Mitsubishi	Dai-Ichi	Sumitomo	Yasuda	Sanwa
June 1931	710	647	659	684	610	–	413	313	371	402	438	–
June 1932	620	616	648	679	607	–	441	344	394	423	460	–
December 1932	687	640	703	735	664	–	429	317	399	447	479	–
June 1933	696	705	769	815	730	–	386	324	406	472	507	–
December 1933	715	661	787	798	740	1025	409	274	418	461	511	519
June 1934	759	696	816	827	800	1063	366	259	409	426	519	489
December 1934	748	722	852	872	807	1077	383	265	422	466	548	496
June 1935	759	752	868	886	818	1080	380	265	432	471	571	494
December 1935	796	730	913	952	832	1114	451	294	448	522	578	494
June 1936	824	805	940	970	891	1151	437	341	450	543	616	526
December 1936	856	810	972	1017	928	1197	518	370	545	618	679	532
June 1937	904	903	1054	1093	1023	1263	531	441	657	691	744	577

Source: Mitsubishi Bank, *Mitsubishi Ginko Shi* (The History of Mitsubishi Bank) (Tokyo: Mitsubishi Bank, 1954) pp. 216–17, 230, 232.

Table 2.6 Mitsui Bank's transactions with Mitsui enterprises, 1937–43 (thousand yen)

	End June 1937		End June 1939		End December 1940		End March 1943	
	Loans	Deposits	Loans	Deposits	Loans	Deposits	Loans	Deposits
Mitsui Gomei	–	–	15 000 (15 270)	5689 (5689)	–	1929	–	–
Mitsui and Company	(38 356)	(22 115)	6578 (53 788)	29 065 (33 131)	84 862 (128 295)	65 667 (68 706)	(137 177)	(84 962)
Mitsui Mining	–	–	12 509 (14 732)	2805 (2806)	29 768 (32 095)	7982 (7985)	(43 425)	(4452)
Toshiba	–	–	2500	1955	10 800	2455	(36 637)	(20 785)
Oji Paper	(13 693)	(4828)	6897 (13 742)	2608 (2608)	24 357 (50 239)	1548 (1552)	(22 831)	(7074)
Toyo Menka	(35 358)	(1671)	1682 (33 372)	973 (1761)	703 (21 929)	3410 (8454)	(17 293)	(1743)
Kanegafuchi Spinning	(71 764)	(11 882)	45 172 (67 496)	7226 (7255)	41 713 (57 859)	8474 (9055)	(67 455)	(12 438)
Nippon Steel	–	–	1325	4239	6250	13 918	(10 309)	(39 043)
Nihon Seifun	–	–	2565 (24 229)	571 (408)	17 441 (17 565)	2345 (2347)	–	–
Onoda Cement	–	–	1691	220	1682	317	–	–
Toyo Koatsu	–	–	13	0	1340	3	(10 540)	(83)
Total A	–	–	104 250	96 962	237 619	157 782	–	–
Total B	–	–	236 296	101 719	325 528	161 411	–	–

Notes: The figures in brackets are taken from Mitsui Bank's Documents on the Bank's Documents on the Bank's Substantial Credit to Customers. Total A is the sum of figures without brackets. Total B is the total sum of all figures of companies that are shown in brackets plus companies that are not shown in brackets.

Sources: Mitsui Bank, 'Monthly Reports of the Bank's Transactions with Mitsui-Related Companies in Loans and Deposits', in Japan Business History Institute (ed.), Historical Materials on Mitsui Bank, vol. 5 (Tokyo: JBHI, 1978), pp. 564–87; Mitsui Bank, Documents on the Mitsui Bank's Substantial Credit to Customers (Sakura Bank archives, unpublished).

Mitsui Bank's merger with Dai-Ichi Bank

After the outbreak of war with China in 1937 Mitsui Bank was faced with a serious shortage of funds. Furthermore it was concerned that its loans to munitions companies would turn into bad debts during the probable postwar recession. To address these problems the bank decided to change in its lending policy drastically, and to this end it would have to set itself free from the Mitsui family's control as the latter would oppose such a change.

The bank not only had to meet the funding requirements of Mitsui affiliates as the bank responsible for the banking affairs of all Mitsui enterprises, but also had to provide loans to munitions companies and to buy government bonds to fulfil the important public role imposed on leading banks. The bank was unable to supply the funds demanded of it, and to solve this problem it formed a syndicate with other banks facing similar difficulties, planned to open as many branches and offices as possible, and eventually decided to prepare for a merger.[25]

With regard to private banks' operation of funds, a number of laws and orders – such as the Law for the Extraordinary Adjustment of Funds of 1937 and the Order Concerning the Operation of Funds by Banks of 1940 – were introduced after the Foreign Exchange Control Law of 1933.

In the new circumstances Mitsui Bank's transactions with Mitsui affiliates changed a great deal. Before outlining these changes we shall examine the reorganization of the Mitsui zaibatsu between 1937 and 1943, when the merger with Dai-Ichi Bank took place.

Mitsui Gomei (a holding company) merged with Mitsui and Company in August 1940 under the latter's name to form Mitsui and Company's shareholding division. (This division was transferred to a newly established holding company Mitsui Honsha in 1944.) Three companies, including Mitsui Chemicals and Mitsui Shipbuilding and Engineering, were added to Mitsui's directly controlled businesses.[26] The following are illustrative of the bank's transactions with Mitsui affiliates in this period. Firstly, loans by the bank to companies directly controlled by Mitsui and trading under its name increased rapidly, particularly its loans to Mitsui and Company, which reached about 140 million yen at the end of March 1943. Secondly, Mitsui Mining, Tokyo Shibaura Electric, the Japan Steel Works, Toyo Koatsu Industries and the Mitsui Chemical Industry, which were beginning to accept orders from the military, joined Oji Paper as the bank's main commercial borrowers. Finally, the bank's loans to Mitsui affiliates (22 companies) reached almost 30 per cent of its total outstanding loans, as compared with approximately 20 per cent in the mid 1930s.[27]

At the beginning of 1938 a merger strategy was worked out by Junshiro Mandai, chairman of Mitsui Bank from 1937–43. This strategy was aimed not only at making the bank Japan's largest, but also at solving the long-standing problem of separating the bank from the Mitsui zaibatsu. The latter had become a matter of great urgency as the war with China meant that Mandai had to prepare for a probable recession after the war's end, just like the recession of 1900–1 that followed the Sino-Japanese War of 1894–95 and the post-World War I recession of 1920. He was concerned that the bank, which had extended huge loans to munitions companies, would be faced with financial difficulties during this recession and that this might lead to the Mitsui family being bankrupted. Mandai also thought that the bank should change its character and deal more with the general public through an extensive network of branches and offices, as with the British commercial bank model.[28]

The question was, would the Mitsui family accept these changes. After consulting Ikeda (a former executive director of Mitsui Bank and former president of Mitsui Gomei), Takahisa Mitsui (the bank's auditor and a partner at Mitsui Gomei) and Takakimi Mitsui (the senior partner at Mitsui Gomei) to obtain their approval of the proposed merger, Mandai presented his plans to the Mitsui family. The latter eventually agreed to the merger, provided the family (through Mitsui Gomei) became the major shareholder and its name lived on in the new banking entity.[29]

It was with Dai-Ichi Bank, one of Japan's five largest banks, that Mitsui Bank wanted to merge. Mitsui Bank asked the governor of the Bank of Japan to mediate between it and Dai-Ichi to smooth the negotiations. However despite Mandai's preparations his proposal was rejected by Dai-Ichi, which was concerned that the Mitsui family's stipulations would result in the virtual takeover of Dai-Ichi by Mitsui Bank. Thus the early attempt at merger failed, and it took several years for the Mitsui family to withdraw its conditions.

We shall now examine another of Mitsui Bank's desperate attempts to resolve its fund shortage, this time by means of loan syndicates for Toyota Motors in 1937 and Mitsui and Company in 1940 and 1942.

Although Toyota Motors was not always officially included among the Mitsui businesses there is no doubt that the company belonged to Mitsui group in the broad sense as it was the most important of Mitsui and Company's affiliates. The amount lent by Mitsui Bank to Toyota increased when the Toyoda family (the family name of Toyota Motors' founder was Toyoda, not Toyota) entered the motor industry in the 1930s. (The Toyodas first established a motor division at the Toyoda Automatic Weaving Machine Works, and several years later, in August 1937, incorporated it as Toyota Motors.) The company was able to raise 30 million yen for capital investment from a loan syndicate consisting of five banks and two trust companies – including Mitsui Bank and the IBJ – just after its incorporation. Previously Mitsui Bank alone had provided loans to the company, but according to Mandai it had become necessary to form the loan syndicate when Toyota Motors' demand for long-term loans exceeded ten million yen.[30]

The loan syndicate for Mitsui and Company was set up a little after the company merged with Mitsui Gomei and started to serve as both a trading company and a holding company, taking over the shareholding functions of Mitsui Gomei in August 1940. This syndicate, which was formed to supply unsecured loans of less than 100 million yen to the company's trading division, consisted of Mitsui Bank, Dai-Ichi Bank and Sumitomo Bank.[31]

The syndicate established at the beginning of 1942 was more interesting in that it was the first to be set up to supply secured loans to the company's shareholding division, which previously only Mitsui Bank and the Mitsui Trust Company (established in 1924 and later renamed the Mitsui Trust and Banking Company) had been allowed to do. This syndicate consisted of Mitsui Bank, the Mitsui Trust Company, Dai-Ichi Bank and Sumitomo Bank.

The rapid growth of Mitsui Bank's loans to Mitsui and Company, especially to the company's shareholding division, put heavy pressure on the bank so its leaders decided to resume the merger negotiations with Dai-Ichi towards the end of 1942. At that point the Mitsui family was forced to withdraw the stipulations it had made earlier, although it insisted that the newly merged bank should continue to provide loans to the Mitsui businesses. In return the Mitsuis promised Dai-Ichi that they would renounce their demand that the merged bank be called Mitsui, and that they would not insist on being major shareholders in it. To ensure that these two promises were honoured Dai-Ichi not only obtained written confirmation of them from Mitsui Bank, with the governor of the Bank of Japan as a witness, but also asked the Ministry of Finance to make them prerequisites for the Ministry's informal approval of the merger.[32]

Mitsui Bank and Dai-Ichi Bank finally merged in March 1943 and the newly established bank, called Teikoku Bank (Teikoku means Imperial in English), started its operations on 1 April 1943. Teikoku duly became Japan's largest bank, with authorized capital of 200 million yen and deposits of 5600 million yen. Chief among its major borrowers were former Mitsui Bank and Dai-Ichi Bank customers.[33] The bank was the first in Japan to be responsible not solely for the banking affairs of zaibatsu-related enterprises but also for the banking affairs of major industries nationwide.

In August 1944 Teikoku Bank merged with Jugo Bank. This increased the bank's authorized capital to 220 million yen and its deposits to seven billion yen.

Summary

In the late 1920s Mitsui Bank began to be troubled by bad debts by companies such as Suzuki and Tokyo Electric Light. However it managed to weather its troubles without changing its conservative lending policy. It retrieved its loans to the Bank of Taiwan and Suzuki very quickly, and it persuaded Tokyo Electric Light to pay off its debt with the proceeds from the sale of corporate bonds underwritten by the bank.

However the debate on its lending policy intensified both inside and outside the bank when it was troubled by an even worse bad debt problem and uncertainty about its creditworthiness during the Showa depression, which started in 1930. Outside the bank, the Ministry of Commerce and Industry was eager for it to reverse its excessively conservative policy and to work closely with industry.

In the 1930s, for the first time the bank began to act as the main bank for some of its major borrowers. Tokyo Electric Light was among these borrowers, even though it was not a Mitsui affiliate. Previously the bank had tried to reduce its extensive loan transactions with the company and in 1927 had sent three business leaders to serve on the company's board of directors. It had eventually been forced to place the company under its supervision in 1930. In October 1932, when Tokyo Electric's failure to convert its domestic bonds (worth 40 million yen) was causing the company financial difficulties and might trigger concern about the bank's creditworthiness, the bank could not avoid assuming the status of quasi main bank of the company. Furthermore, by forming underwriting syndicates for the company's bonds in 1934–35, the bank succeeded in reducing the amount owed by the company.

After the outbreak of war with China in 1937, the bank not only had to meet the borrowing requirements of Mitsui affiliates, but also had to provide loans to non-affiliated munitions companies and buy government bonds. The bank was unable to supply the funds demanded of it, so in 1938 it began to work out a merger strategy that would not only make it Japan's largest bank, but would also separate the bank from the Mitsui zaibatsu. In 1943 it merged with Dai-Ichi Bank and became Teikoku Bank.

3
Teikoku Bank's New Strategy, 1943–45

When Teikoku Bank started operations in April 1943 it adopted a policy of offering long-term capital loans over one-year period, as well as underwriting and holding corporate bonds. Supplying funds for production expansion in line with the national goals, an expression contained in a slogan of the time, meant the same thing as extending long-term capital loans.[1] The bank's main objective was to secure business that had long been mainly the preserve of the Industrial Bank of Japan.[2] Large banks such as Sumitomo and Yasuda were still cautious of offering long-term loans, yet at the same time they were envious of Teikoku Bank's success in doing so. Kenzo Oshima, the executive managing director of Sumitomo Bank, said at a meeting in October 1943 that the rise in major industries' demand for funds had led to a large increase in bank lending, and that most of this lending involved long-term capital loans that were essentially unsuitable for deposit banks.[3] On the other hand, in a history of Yasuda Bank it is stated that although the bank made a positive effort to increase its long-term capital loans, the three largest zaibatsu, including Mitsui, had built such a close relationship with promising munitions companies that it was difficult for Yasuda Bank to engage with these companies.[4]

The plan to enter long-term capital lending

In the second half of 1943 the identification of priority industries and companies was introduced into the government's industrial policy, and as a result industry-to-industry and company-to-company

differences widened quickly.[5] While this partly resolved the large
bank's fund shortage problem by reducing the demand for funds for
low priority industries, large banks such as Teikoku still faced serious
shortages and were therefore forced to abandon their plans to provide long-term loans to industry. This was the first time that large
banks had depended on the government for public funds. Teikoku's
fund shortage became evident at the end of June 1943 when its
accounting term ended. At that time the bank had to borrow 150
million yen from the Bank of Japan to purchase the government
bonds that had been allocated to it.[6]

A memorandum by the bank's managing director dated 4 August
shows that the bank was forced to resume its restrictive lending policy and make a greater effort to attract deposits. One of several possible remedial approaches was to hand over to government financial
institutions certain kinds of loan that were unsuitable for Teikoku
as a private commercial bank.[7] At a branch managers' meeting in
November 1943, when the fund shortage had become even more
serious, the bank's president, Junshiro Mandai, appealed to those
present to think about the problem and suggest measures to make
the restrictive lending policy more effective. A measure subsequently
adopted was loan prioritization in correspondence with the priority
principle introduced by the government for manufacturing industries.[8] To facilitate this, in December 1943 the bank asked the
government to introduce a system of obliging banks to make preferential loans to companies designated by the government as important to the war effort (*Gunju Yushi Shitei Kinyukikan Seido*). As will be
discussed later, Teikoku gradually became the designated bank for
more than 170 munitions companies.

In spite of the bank's various measures to resolve its fund shortage, its borrowings from the Bank of Japan continued to increase.
This was partly because all the large banks were competing to
become the designated bank for as many priority munitions companies as possible,[9] and partly because most of the munitions companies that were having difficulty obtaining advances on sales
contracts from the government pulled their deposits out of the
banks (at the government's instruction) during the final stages of
the war.[10]

After January 1944 Teikoku intensified its loan prioritization and
continued to ask the Industrial Bank of Japan to provide long-term

funds to the designated munitions companies that the bank had made its prime borrowers. It was not until a new law guaranteed an exclusive or close relationship between the bank and these companies that the bank was able to extend its strategy on a large scale, and in so doing guard itself against the IBJ penetrating its customer base. The crucial point here is that the bank was obliged to become too dependent on the IBJ's funds, which was potentially harmful to its long-term lending business.

In January 1944 the government identified 150 major companies as important to the war effort and Teikoku became the designated bank for 49 of these companies: the main designee for 47 companies and subdesignee for two companies. As Table 3.1 shows, the classification 'main designee' was divided into two types: sole designee and codesignee with other banks. The IBJ and Teikoku were codesignees for 20 companies, including Tokyo Shibaura Electric, Toyota Motors, Toyo Koatsu, Mitsui Shipbuilding and Engineering, Mitsui Chemical Industry, Hitachi and Furukawa Denko. The bank was sole designee for Kawasaki Heavy Industries and its two sister companies, which were former Dai-Ichi Bank customers. In this way Kawasaki Heavy Industries became one of the largest users of Teikoku's funds, alongside Mitsui and Company, during the final stages of the war.[11]

Under the new system the banks used by each munitions company were supposed to be unified into a single bank called the designated bank, but in most cases a commercial bank and the IBJ were chosen as codesignees. Predictably the problem arose of which of the two codesignees would maintain the closer relationship with the

Table 3.1 Designated banks of 150 major munitions companies, 1944

| | Main designee | | | |
	Sole designee	Codesignee	Total	Subdesignee
IBJ	3	60	63	0
Teikoku	22	25	47	2
Sumitomo	10	15	25	1
Mitsubishi	12	11	23	1
Yasuda	2	14	16	1
Sanwa	5	9	14	1

Source: Sumitomo Bank, *Sumitomo Ginko 80-nen Shi* (The 80 Year History of Sumitomo Bank) (Osaka: Sumitomo Bank, 1979), p. 332.

company. According to a memorandum dated 18 February 1944 from the head of the department that screened loan applications at Teikoku Bank, the bank was not in a position to secure the superior place.[12] This suggests that the bank's fund shortage problem was serious enough to allow the IBJ to form a close relationship with the customers as a guard against Teikoku Bank. As it turned out, however, Teikoku need not have worried about the IBJ's offensive[13] because the munitions industry's demand for long-term capital funds declined sharply after 1944.

Borrowing requirements, 1941–45

Collectively, financial institutions' outstanding loans to the manufacturing industry from the end of December 1941 to the end of March 1945 rose from 43.9 per cent to 51.6 per cent of total outstanding loans. Loans to the machinery industry, to which most munitions companies belonged, reached 15 440 million yen or 30.0 per cent of total outstanding loans at the end of March 1945. As can be seen in Table 3.2, between the end of December 1943 and the end of March 1945, the greatest proportion of these loans was used as working funds. The increase in loans for working funds in the machinery industry outnumbered the increase in long-term capital loans by a ratio of four to one, compared with three to one between the end of June 1940 and the end of 1943.

There were similar trends in the lending operations of individual large banks such as Teikoku and Mitsubishi, although there is insufficient information to come to a definite conclusion. (We are forced to use Teikoku Bank information to illustrate the large banks' lending operations before the end of 1943 and Mitsubishi Bank information to illustrate their lending operations thereafter.) Teikoku's outstanding loans at the end of June 1943 amounted to 3264 million yen, consisting mainly of 2051 million yen for working funds and 338 million yen for long-term loans. Its outstanding loans at the end of September 1943 amounted to 3756 million yen, including 2279 million yen for working funds and 468 million yen for long-term loans.[14] This shows that the increase in the loans provided by the bank as working funds outnumbered the increase in long-term loans by a ratio of approximately three to one during these three months. On the other hand, the loans provided by Mitsubishi Bank

55

Table 3.2 Outstanding loans to the manufacturing and machinery industries, all financial institutions, 1940-45 (million yen)

	Manufacturing industry				Machinery industry			
	Long-term loans		Working funds		Long-term loans		Working funds	
	(Amount)	(Index)	(Amount)	(Index)	(Amount)	(Index)	(Amount)	(Index)
End June 1940	1616	100	3170	100	542	100	936	100
End December 1941	2144	132	4424	139	874	161	1536	164
End December 1942	2512	155	5420	170	986	181	2135	228
End December 1943	3597	222	7543	237	1778	328	3406	363
End March 1945	6675	413	17990	567	3588	661	11268	1203

Source: Industrial Bank of Japan, *The 50 Year History of the Industrial Bank of Japan* (Tokyo: Industrial Bank of Japan, 1957), p. 535.

as working funds to the designated munitions companies out-weighed long-term loans by a ratio of more than six to one during the period March 1944 to March 1945.

Summary

Teikoku Bank, established in 1943 following the merger of Mitsui Bank and Dai-Ichi Bank, was the first Japanese bank to be responsible for the banking affairs of major industries nationwide. Among the bank's plans was to offer long-term capital loans over one-year period for war production, in line with the national goals. However it began to face a serious fund shortage at the end of June 1943, just three months after the start of its operations, and was therefore forced to abandon its expansion of long-term lending.

After January 1944 the bank intensified its loan prioritization but had to ask the IBJ to provide long-term loans to the munitions companies that it had made its prime borrowers. It was not until a new law guaranteed an exclusive or close relationship between Teikoku and these companies that the bank was able to pursue its strategy on a large scale and act as the quasi main bank of munitions companies, including 47 major ones, for which it became main designee.

4
Formation of the Mitsui Group through Loan Relationships, 1945–60

Thanks to the forced dissolution of the zaibatsu immediately after the war, Teikoku Bank and other zaibatsu-affiliated banks were freed from the control of the zaibatsu families. As a result, all of them became able to act as lender of last resort for major companies at their own discretion.

In the postwar years Japan's six largest commercial banks – mainly the former zaibatsu-affiliated banks – abandoned their policy of keeping their borrowing customers at arm's length and concentrated on grouping together the largest and most promising of their customers and serving as their main bank. Six such corporate groupings, headed by the banks, came into existence in the early 1950s. In order to carry out this policy successfully it was essential for them to offer long-term capital loans. However they instead tended to emphasize the provision of short-term loans and the discounting of commercial bills of exchange, especially foreign ones, through increased transactions with the major trading companies. In particular they tried to increase their share of loans to wholesalers in order to balance their loan composition by industry. In order to focus on the provision of short-term loans they asked other financial institutions to share the burden of providing long-term capital funds to their customers, and in this way they partly met the demand for long-term loans by their customers in the heavy and chemical industries.

This situation also provided a stimulus for the formation of company groups, both as a means to put loan prioritization into practice and as a guard against the poaching of customers by other financial institutions.

Set free from the Mitsui family

After the end of the Pacific War on 15 August 1945 Japan was placed under the control of the allied occupation forces, a situation that continued until 28 April 1952. During this occupation the demilitarization and democratization of Japan was carried out. The former meant dismantling the armed forces, closing the armaments factories and purging the public service of wartime officials. The dissolution of the zaibatsu was among the various policies adopted in the interest of democratization. Fifteen zaibatsu, including Mitsui, Mitsubishi, Sumitomo and Yasuda, were dismantled and prohibited from using their company names or trademarks. In 1947 laws were enacted to ban holding companies, break up monopoly corporations and prevent the reemergence of zaibatsu.

Emergency financial measures were introduced to curb rising prices and reconstruct the economy. Government and private funds were directed towards key industries, such as coal and steel, in the hope that growth in these basic industries would stimulate growth in the rest of the economy. In 1948 a nine-point programme for economic stabilization and inflation control was adopted. In 1949 the Dodge Plan, which called for a strictly balanced budget and the pegging of the yen exchange rate at 360 yen per US dollar, was put into effect. Although inflation was arrested by this strong deflationary medicine, the economy fell into recession.

Recovery in the banking sector was somewhat more rapid than in other sectors. The former zaibatsu-affiliated banks were forced to change their names but not to segment. They were essentially back on their feet by the autumn of 1948, despite the cessation of the government's wartime incentive payments. With the dissolution in 1948 of the Reconstruction Finance Bank (which had been an important source of reconstruction funds for industry, but also a prime contributor to inflation), Japan's major commercial banks took on the task of financing reconstruction, but this led them into an excess loan situation. During this period the former zaibatsu banks tended to act as the nucleus of enterprises that had previously belonged to the zaibatsu, and as such became essential players in the reconstruction of the economy.[1] The major banks' excess loan situation suggests that they had begun to take on much more responsibility for the banking affairs of their customers than before, although this was obligatory rather than voluntary.

On 1 October 1948 Yasuda Bank began operations under the name of Fuji Bank, and Teikoku Bank was redivided into Mitsui Bank and Dai-Ichi Bank. Prior to this the banks had presented to the minister of finance their plans for meeting the Financial Institutions' Reorganization and Readjustment Law (*Kinyu Kikan Saiken Seibi Ho*), and these plans had been approved.

During the period of rapid economic growth (1955–73) Mitsubishi Bank outstripped the other major banks in grouping around itself the largest and most promising trade and manufacturing customers. However it was Fuji Bank rather than Mitsubishi Bank that served as a top bank before and during the early stage of this growth. More specifically, Fuji Bank seemed to conduct itself like predivided Teikoku Bank before 1948 in case one of the three other major commercial banks consisting of Mitsui, Mitsubishi and Sumitomo or the IBJ showed a keen interest in the plan which Fuji tried to advocate. This was because Fuji was not overwhelmingly predominant among the major banks. In this situation Mitsui Bank and the IBJ were invaluable to Fuji as collaborators, particularly in respect of carrying out its plan to resolve their fund shortages.

Fuji Bank's leadership over the other major banks was first manifest in its aggressive policy to increase its share of trade financing. (It is important to note that during the reconstruction period Japan's major banks moulded their character on the struggle for increased share of trade financing.) Fuji's ties with trading companies had not been particularly strong before the Pacific War, but it recognized the importance of trade for postwar Japan and was determined to strengthen its relationships with such companies. With the plentiful resources it enjoyed as Japan's number one bank, in 1948 it increased its financing of trade bills as much as five fold in the short space of ten months, thus securing its place at the top of the major bank league.

At the end of fiscal year 1946 the average ratio of loans to deposits for the largest banks had risen to 124.5 per cent, compared with 93.3 per cent a year earlier – vicious inflation and monetary uncertainty was making it extremely difficult for the banks to attract deposits. The average ratio rose a further 100 per cent or more in 1949. That year supplementary credit was granted to private banks by the Bank of Japan as part of the government's disinflation policy to offset the extremely balanced budget under the Dodge Plan.

After the outbreak of the Korean War in June 1950 the United Nations Armed Forces began to purchase Japanese goods and services. This brought about a procurement boom, but with the general retrenchment of arms expansion in 1951 this boom tapered off, the commodity market deteriorated, a number of trading companies and textile wholesalers collapsed, and the banks' excess loan problem continued.[2]

Under the economic prosperity of the boom period a special law was enacted to encourage key industries to increase their efficiency by modernizing their equipment. This prompted extensive capital investment by the four priority industries – electric power, shipping, iron and steel, and coal mining – as well as fertilizers, synthetic fibres, shipbuilding and electrical machinery. Enterprises hungry for capital rushed to the banks. Their demand for funds far outstripped the growth in deposits, and so the banks were forced to fill the gap by borrowing from the Bank of Japan.[3]

Mitsui Bank's complicated relationship with Mitsui and Company

After the enactment in December 1947 of the Law for the Elimination of Excessive Concentration of Economic Power (*Kado Keizairyoku Shuchuhaijo Ho*), it was perceived that the law would be applied to banks as well as business companies. In anticipation of this, former members of Dai-Ichi Bank submitted a request to the president of Teikoku Bank, Kiichiro Sato (who had assumed the presidency in 1946 and held real power over the bank's management), to divide the bank into its former components.

Under the stipulation imposed by SCAP (the Supreme Commander for the Allied Powers) that separation should be conducted equitably between all the parties to the original merger, the branches and personnel of the former Jugo Bank were to join forces with Mitsui Bank. At the end of September 1948 Teikoku was dissolved and its business was transferred to two newly established banks: Dai-Ichi Bank and 'new' Teikoku Bank.[4] Although new Teikoku did not revert to the name Mitsui Bank until 1 January 1954, we shall refer to it throughout as Mitsui Bank for the sake of convenience.

When Mitsui Bank made its fresh start on 1 October 1948 it was capitalized at 950 million yen, had deposits of 20.2 billion yen, loans receivable of 15.4 billion yen and loans payable of 6.3 billion yen. When it separated from Dai-Ichi Bank it lost half its branch network and half its funds. It had only 85 branches and was obliged to continue to provide funds to Mitsui-affiliated companies and a wide range of other customers.[5]

In the meantime Mitsui and Company, which in prewar days had been known worldwide as Japan's largest trading company, was dissolved into more than 200 separate companies in July 1947 by SCAP. Daiichi Bussan, Daiichi Trading, Goyo Boeki Kaisha, Nippon Kikai Boeki, Kokusai Bussan, Ocean Trading, Toho Bussan Kaisha and Muromachi Bussan were among the new companies to emerge from Mitsui and Company's dissolution. Of these Daiichi Trading, established in February 1949 upon the merger of Daiichi Boeki and Nippon Tsusho, was initially the most prominent company and nucleus of the corporate structure from which Mitsui Bank expected the new Mitsui and Company to emerge. The company operated as a general trading company and absorbed several prominent companies as it grew.[6]

Daiichi Bussan was destined eventually to become Mitsui's nucleus, but Mitsui Bank did not rate the company as highly as Daiichi Trading until about 1951. That was why the bank asked Fuji Bank to share the burden of providing funds to Daiichi Bussan while maintaining a close relationship with the company as its main bank. Thus Fuji Bank, whose fund shortage problem was not as serious as Mitsui Bank's, became the main creditor of Daiichi Bussan until the early 1950s (Tables 4.1 and 4.2). It would have also become the main bank of Daiichi Bussan if general panic had not gripped the trading companies and countermeasures had not been taken against this eventuality by Mitsui Bank.

The 100 Year History of Mitsui & Co. describes the company's close relationship with Fuji Bank. It is stated in this book that Fuji Bank was Daiichi Bussan's main bank for many years, replacing Mitsui Bank, which had not shown a particular interest in providing loans to the company, and that Fuji and Daiichi Bussan were in mutually complementary positions in that Fuji wanted to expand its foreign exchange business, which was weak because Fuji had had no prewar association with a prominent trading company, and Daiichi Bussan

Table 4.1 Banks' short-term loans to the successors of Mitsui and Company, September 1953 (million yen)

Bank	Daiichi Bussan	Daiichi Trading	(Former) Mitsui & Co.	Nippon Kikai Boeki Kaisha	General Bussan	Total	%
Kangyo	–	191	18	390	–	601	2.4
IBJ	587	–	–	810	–	1397	5.6
Bank of Tokyo	1281	1924	89	287	–	3584	14.4
Mitsui	1701	2686	684	1143	537	6752	27.1
Mitsubishi	542	88	–	–	–	630	2.5
Sumitomo	505	68	57	743	–	1375	5.5
Fuji	2746	897	121	54	20	3839	15.4
Dai-Ichi	431	174	197	224	–	1027	4.1
Sanwa	298	326	3	90	–	718	2.9
Daiwa	364	153	7	–	–	524	2.1
Kobe	366	63	–	136	–	566	2.3
Tokai	62	224	–	225	30	543	2.2
Kyowa	–	–	15	10	43	68	0.3
Mitsui Trust	342	67	99	–	58	567	2.3
Mitsubishi Trust	115	–	–	–	28	143	0.6
Sumitomo Trust	161	13	–	–	–	174	0.7
Mitsui Life	–	–	–	16	–	16	0.1
Others	1063	463	21	380	435	2363	9.5
Total	10570	7342	1316	4514	1152	24896	100.0

Source: Research Division, Economic Planning Agency, 'Shuyo Boekishosha Bunseki Shiryo (Documents on Major Trading Companies)', in National Institute for Research Advancement (ed.), Keizai Antei Hombu Sengo Keizai Seisaku Shiryo (Documents on the Postwar Economic Policy of Economic Planning Agency and its Predecessors), vol. 27 (Tokyo: Nihon Keizai Hyoronsha, 1995), pp. 32–3.

Table 4.2 The main sources of short-term loans to Daiichi Bussan, 1951–58 (million yen)

End September 1951		End September 1958	
Source	*Amount*	*Source*	*Amount*
Fuji Bank	570	Mitsui Bank	5828
Mitsui Trust	361	Fuji Bank	4262
Mitsui Bank	250	Bank of Tokyo	3824
Daiwa Bank	240	Sumitomo Bank	2334
Bank of Tokyo	238	Nippon Kangyo Bank	1707
Yasuda Trust	159	Sanwa Bank	1582
Mitsui Bank	138	Dai-Ichi Bank	816
Hokkaido Takushoku Bank	101	IBJ	709
Saitama Bank	98	Hokkaido Takushoku Bank	683
Bank of Yokohama	80	Mitsubishi Bank	627
Total, including other sources	2659	Total, including other sources	24 518

Source: Mitsui and Company, *The 100 Year History of Mitsui & Co. Ltd. 1876–1976* (English edition) (Tokyo: Mitsui & Co., 1977), p. 202. Reprinted with permission.

wanted an affiliation with a powerful financial institution in order to raise funds.[7]

Between 1951 and 1958, however, as Table 4.2 shows, Mitsui Bank took the lead over Fuji in respect of providing short-term loans to Daiichi Bussan. This came about because Daiichi Bussan annexed many companies related to the old Mitsui and Company – companies that had been heavily financed by Mitsui Bank – and because of the bank's change in policy to positive support of Daiichi Bussan: it had become evident to everyone that Daiichi Bussan was the leading light among the companies that had emerged from the dissolution of Mitsui and Company. In addition, after the spring of 1952, when most trading companies were heavily damaged by the general panic and the ban on using zaibatsu names was lifted, Daiichi Bussan changed its approach to Mitsui Bank and asked the latter to become its main creditor. It also wanted to retrieve the name 'Mitsui and Company'.

Mitsui Bank's foreign-exchange-oriented lending policy

In the immediate postwar years the large Japanese banks, including Mitsui Bank, were keen to increase their long-term capital lending business, and as government financial institutions had been banned by SCAP there was a good opportunity for them to do so. In practice, however, the fact that they continued to experience serious fund shortages prevented them from doing so to any significant degrees, so instead they rushed to reestablish their foreign exchange business by increasing their transactions with trading companies.

Before discussing Mitsui Bank's reestablishment of its foreign exchange business we shall glance at its fund shortage problem. When the government halted the issuing of new loans by the Reconstruction Finance Bank, as recommended in the Dodge economic programme, Japan's largest commercial banks had to take responsibility for the loans that had already been promised for capital goods and equipment. In 1949, when non-financial corporations depended on banks for 47.9 per cent of the funds they borrowed for investment in plant and facilities, Mitsui Bank increased the amount of its loans by 18.78 billion yen, while its deposits rose by 18.31 billion yen. In September 1949 loans receivable were equal to 81 per cent of the amount of deposits and by March 1950 they had increased to 92 per cent. The bank had to borrow more heavily from the Bank of Japan than other banks did because it had many major corporations as customers, and the bank's excess loan problem became increasingly more serious as the demand grew for long-term funds for priority industries, the repair and overhaul of equipment and the rationalization programmes.[8]

It is clear that the government's request to the large banks, including Mitsui Bank, to share the burden of providing long-term capital loans to industry caused them a serious fund shortage problem. But, taking Teikoku Bank's behavior during the war into account, we can see that originally the banks asked government financial institutions such as the Industrial Bank of Japan to share the burden of providing long-term capital funds to their customers. It is clear that large banks were unable to solve by themselves their fund shortage problem and establish a long-term capital lending business. And thereafter the problem continued to be perceived in this way for a long time. In fact, as a restrictive lending policy, Mitsui Bank decided to ask other financial institutions including governmental ones, to share the burden of providing funds to its customers again. In addition, it set loan ceilings for each of its branches, imposed stricter conditions for granting loans and so on, and made special efforts to attract deposits.[9]

Compared with long-term capital lending, foreign exchange was less of a headache for Mitsui Bank, in spite of its fund shortage problem. This was also true for most of Japan's other large banks. Export trade was restored to the private sector in December 1949, and import business was restored in January 1950. Mitsui Bank was designated as a first-grade foreign exchange bank by the Ministry of Finance in November 1949, alongside other large banks such as Mitsubishi, Dai-Ichi, Daiwa, Kobe, Nihon Kangyo, Sumitomo, Sanwa, Tokai and Tokyo (the successor to the Yokohama Specie Bank). In this capacity Mitsui Bank was authorized to conclude business agreements with equivalent banks overseas, and in 1950 it forged agreements with the National City Bank of New York, the Chase National Bank of the City of New York, the Bank of America National Trust and Savings Association, the Bankers Trust Company, the Bank of the Manhattan and the Chemical Bank and Trust Company.[10]

According to the report of a branch managers' meeting in July 1950, the bank thought that the business could be made profitable with a relatively small amount of funds, but that for the six months ending 30 September the Bank of Tokyo would turn four times as much profit and Fuji Bank and Sumitomo Bank twice as much profit on their foreign exchange business as Mitsui Bank.[11] That foreign exchange business became so attractive to a number of Japan's largest banks during the recovery period and even during the early stages of the period of high-speed growth was due mainly to the government's policy of helping them to make profit in this field. More specifically, the government protected them by restricting the number of foreign exchange banks authorized under the Foreign Exchange and Foreign Trade Control Law (*Gaikoku Kawase oyobi Gaikoku Boeki Kanri Ho*) to conduct foreign exchange business.

SCAP's occupation policies began to shift from the demilitarization and democratization of Japan to its rapid reconstruction and independence in late 1948, when the Cold War started. A small number of large banks were expected to play an important role in the reconstruction of the economy, which is why banks were not

Table 4.3   The 12 largest commercial banks' loan compositions, by industry, 1951–53 (million yen)

| | End March 1951 | | | | End March 1953 | | | |
| | Mitsui Bank | | Other 11 banks | | Mitsui Bank | | Other 11 banks | |
	(Amount)	(%)	(Amount)	(%)	(Amount)	(%)	(Amount)	(%)
Manufacturing	26755	52.62	314199	53.59	49873	42.89	599863	48.54
Cotton spinning	5654	11.12	60450	10.30	8932	7.68	113890	9.21
Chemicals	5064	9.95	41475	7.07	9053	7.78	69166	5.59
Steel	1554	3.05	29063	4.95	5015	4.31	79671	6.44
Machinery	7110	13.98	57700	9.83	9842	8.46	93655	7.57
Mining	5176	10.18	19525	3.32	8675	7.46	33526	2.71
Coal	4854	9.54	15775	2.68	5986	5.14	22413	1.81
Commerce	11776	23.16	175416	29.90	43564	37.46	452086	36.58
Wholesale	11266	22.15	167593	28.57	42772	36.78	437086	35.37
(Trading companies)	(4532)	(8.91)	–	–	(23941)	(20.58)	–	–
Retail	510	1.00	7823	1.33	792	0.68	15000	1.21
Public utilities	3269	6.42	34109	5.81	7939	6.82	78140	6.32
Shipping	1465	2.88	15614	2.66	3378	2.90	40297	3.26
Electricity	581	1.14	3224	0.54	2383	2.04	14871	1.20
Gas	819	1.61	4936	0.84	1015	0.87	5904	0.47
Subtotal	46976	92.39	543249	92.62	110051	94.64	1163615	94.16
Others	3868	7.60	43245	7.37	6224	5.35	72102	5.83
(Construction)	(93.3)	(1.83)	(11336)	(1.93)	(1412)	(1.21)	(18117)	(1.46)
Total	50844	100.00	586494	100.00	116275	100.00	1235717	100.00

Source: Mitsui Bank, 'Directives on Loan Screening from the 9th Branch Managers' Meeting', in 'Records of Mitsui Bank's Branch Managers' Meetings' (unpublished).

made subject to the Law for the Elimination of Excessive Concentration of Economic Power, even though it had been expected that the law would be applied to banks as well as corporations immediately after the war.[12]

Despite the government's protection of foreign exchange business, banks were forced to focus on the provision of short-term loans to companies while reducing their long-term loans and forming a balanced loan composition by industry. It can be deduced from Table 4.3 that Mitsui and 11 other large banks were eager to increase their loans to wholesalers (mainly trading companies). Loans to wholesalers were mostly short term, and banks still suffering from fund shortages engaged in cutthroat competition to secure the business of prominent companies.

Mitsui Bank soon became aware that there was a strong correlation between the provision of short-term loans to trading companies and doing foreign exchange business with them. For example a bank's ranking among the purchases of trading companies' export bills was greatly influenced by the loans on trade bills it provided to them. The same was not necessarily true of the settlement of import bills, so Mitsui Bank tried to make up for its handicap in buying export bills by increasing the amount of import bills it settled, such as bills for importing iron ore, coking coal, food, rubber, hides and soya beans.[13]

In autumn 1953, when the balance of payments deficit drastically worsened because of an increase in imports (reflecting improved prosperity) the government introduced tight monetary and fiscal policies. These policies not only caused most banks, headed by Mitsui Bank, to introduce strict loan prioritization, but also triggered the recession of 1954, so ending the boom that followed the recession that followed the Korean War boom in 1950. The economy continued to fluctuate like this until the 1960s. For Mitsui Bank the decision to put loan prioritization into practice was a significant one, as will be discussed later.

The reestablishment of Mitsui and Company

Many Japanese trading companies were heavily damaged by the post-Korean War recession. In particular, deficits resulting from speculative imports of three new commodities – rubber, hides and soya beans – combined with cancellations from overseas of textile export contracts to cause irreparable damage to traders. According to a Fair Trade Commission estimate, traders' total losses amounted to about 21 363 million yen at the end of March 1952. The losses they incurred from the sudden drop in the prices of the three new commodities amounted to 6357 million yen, or about 30 per cent of their total losses. Though on the whole they suffered heavier damage from the fall in the prices of cotton yarn and cotton cloth than they did from the fall in the prices of the three new commodities, most of the trading companies that had emerged from the old Mitsui and Company were hurt more by the latter. More specifically, 40 of the 70 largest trading companies suffered losses of about 5500 million yen. Large trading companies specializing in cotton, such as C. Itoh and Marubeni, were among the companies bearing the brunt. Conversely, general traders or those specializing in metals either made a profit or managed to ride out the crisis, which prompted C. Itoh, Marubeni and others to move towards general trading by buying companies specializing in steel and other products.[14]

Interestingly, a disparity in the performance of different trading companies was evident not only during this recession but also during the recession of 1954 and the lingering recession of 1958. The same held true of the new companies founded by former employees of Mitsui and Company and others after its dissolution. The Daiichi Trading Company was particularly hard hit by the post-Korean War recession. This company merged on equal terms with Sanshin Seni Boeki and Kyokuto Bussan in January 1953 to form a new company, also called the Daiichi Trading Company, but the losses incurred prior to the merger were so large that it was taken over by Daiichi Bussan in July 1955.[15]

Crucial here are the size of the new Daiichi Trading Company's loss and the extent to which Mitsui and other banks wrote off or postponed repayment of the debts incurred by the company. These banks invested heavily in the success of Daiichi Trading's merger with Daiichi Bussan and Nippon Kikai Boeki:

> Daiichi Bussan's negotiations with Daiichi Trading, Nippon Kikai Boeki and the former Mitsui & Co. entered their final stages after the conclusion of the merger with Mitsui Lumber. The most difficult problems involved Daiichi Trading, already a major trading company second in scale only to Daiichi Bussan among the

companies related to the old Mitsui & Co., but in serious management trouble.

There could be no true reunification of the companies related to the old Mitsui & Co. if Daiichi Trading were not included. The Mitsui, Tokyo and Fuji Banks felt particularly strongly about that point for they had provided Daiichi Trading with extensive relief loans.

As the positions of Daiichi Bussan, Nippon Kikai Boeki, Daiichi Trading and their banks were relatively close, a merger proposal was drafted. Tatsuzo Mizukami and representatives of the banks played key roles in preparing the draft. The final plan showed it was possible to dispose of Daiichi Trading's losses by combining a decrease in capitalization with a later issue of new shares for offsetting its liabilities. The latter method had worked well with Goyo Boeki.[16]

As Muromachi Bussan did not participate in the 1955 merger, the latter has been called the 'three main companies' consolidation' to differentiate it from 'the grand merger' of 1959 between Daiichi Bussan and Muromachi Bussan to form the new Mitsui and Company.

As will be discussed later, the large-scale loan prioritization introduced after the recession of 1954 was a reproduction of that implemented during World War II under the system of obliging banks to make preferential loans to companies designated by the government as important to the war effort. In wartime the designated banks were not only the major munitions companies' main banks but also their main creditors, without exception. When designating the banks the government took into account their transactions with the munitions companies for the past five years, including loans, as a close relationship between the banks and the companies was vital if loan prioritization was to be successful.

The principle that the main bank of a company must be its main creditor held even more true during the period of loan prioritization in the mid 1950s. Hence serving as the principal creditor of Daiichi Bussan, which was to become the main corporate structure from which Mitsui and Company would re-emerge, was essential to Fuji Bank. Likewise Mitsui Bank needed to play a leading role if it was to re-establish itself as Mitsui and Company's main bank. This conflict of interests between main bank and main creditor caused a serious but not insurmountable negotiating impasse in Daiichi Bussan's pursuit of mergers with Daiichi Trading and other companies.

The success or failure of these mergers depended decisively on the extent to which the banks concerned were willing to write off their loans to Daiichi Trading, or on the extent to which Daiichi Bussan reduced the liabilities inherited from Daiichi Trading by obtaining these banks' cooperation. Mitsui Bank assessed Daiichi Trading's deficits at 3286 million yen, based on the company's results for the six months ending 30 September 1953. At that time the company's total outstanding relief loans from the banking syndicate composed of Mitsui, Tokyo, Fuji and Sanwa was 3200 million yen, and this figure had been used as the basis upon which to assess the company's deficits. Mitsui Bank was of the opinion that each of the four banks' share of debt write-off should be proportionate to the size of its relief loans to the company. The other banks did not agree, but they managed to work out a compromise in March 1955.

Under the compromise arrangement Daiichi Bussan would repay about 88 per cent of the liabilities it had inherited from Daiichi Trading by issuing new shares. This was an ingenious way of resolving the credit problem in that although it would mean the banks would have to write off just under 80 per cent of their loans when calculated at double the face value of the shares, an increase in the price of the company's shares would allow repayment of a considerable proportion of the loans. Even though this proved to be the case, the disposal of the company's deficits caused serious temporary damage to the banks. Of the 3286 million yen deficit, 400 million yen was converted into long-term loans to Daiichi Bussan, which was to take over the business of Daiichi Trading, and 600 million yen was exchanged for six million new shares in Daiichi Bussan. The remaining 2286 million yen was written off. Mitsui Bank's share of this write-off was 65.3 per cent.[17]

Loan prioritization, 1953–55

Proper examination reveals that Mitsui Bank's move to establish a Mitsui-affiliated group of trading companies through loan relationships was a prerequisite for the implementation of its strict loan prioritization policy, and that this move was not unique to Mitsui Bank.

Prior to this episode of loan prioritization there were two earlier examples: one during the war years, as discussed previously, and another during the Allied Powers' occupation. In the case of the latter, the Ministry of Finance laid down 'Rules Concerning Loans by Financial Institutions' in March 1947. These rules stipulated, among other things, that financial institutions should provide loans to industries according to their designated order of importance. Under the so-called 'priority production' system, whereby steel, coal mining and a small number of other important industries were to be supplied with raw materials, funds and labour on a priority basis so that they could operate regular production schedules.[18]

The loan prioritization implemented during the mid 1950s differed from its predecessors in that it did not move in accordance with government financial measures. Rather the banks were urged to push on with it themselves, and the prioritization was stricter and its scale larger.

The individual banks divided their customers into two categories: affiliated companies, for which they acted as main banks as well as main creditors; and non-affiliated companies under other banks' influence. Because of their fund shortages they asked other financial institutions to share the burden of providing funds to the former, while diminishing or cutting off transactions with the latter.[19] Hence the banks favoured the members of their own business groups, or to be more precise, they first formed affiliated groups through loan relationships and then selected a small number of the largest and the most promising companies from the affiliated groups to become members of their business groups. Trading companies, particularly the less promising ones, suddenly had their loans called in by creditors other than their main bank.

According to a Fair Trade Commission investigation, there had been affiliations between prominent trading companies and Japan's five largest banks and the Bank of Tokyo at the end of September 1953, just before the loan prioritization was implemented. This investigation also revealed the existence of particular types of transaction and relationship between them, such as loans, cross-share-holdings and shared directorships. Daiichi Bussan, Daiichi Trading, Mitsui and Company (Muromachi Bussan), Nippon Kikai Boeki, Tokyo Food Products (later renamed Toshoku), General Bussan and Toyo Menka (a subsidiary company of the old Mitsui and Company) were judged quite accurately by the Commission to be affiliated trading companies of Mitsui Bank, but Daiichi Bussan, Daiichi Trading and Toyo Menka were also deemed to be associate members of Fuji Bank's affiliated trading companies. Fuji and Sanwa Banks' affiliated trading companies had several associate members. Marubeni was affiliated to Sumitomo Bank until September 1953, when Fuji Bank succeeded in becoming its main bank and getting it to merge with Takashimaya Iida under the control of Fuji Bank.[20]

We shall now turn our attention to how Mitsui Bank put loan prioritization into practice. According to the record of a branch managers' meeting in January 1954, the bank found itself in the awkward position of being obliged to reduce its loans to customers amid an intense demand for money. The shortfall between the increase in the bank's outstanding loans and the increase in its deposits (the former outweighing the latter, Table 4.4) during the nine months from the end of March 1953 to the end of the year was largest among the major banks. Consequently, the bank considered that in principle any increase in the funds supplied for loans, foreign exchange and securities investment should be restricted to the increase in real deposits. This suggests that the bank had almost reached the point where it would not be able to extend new loans to its customers.

Having tried unsuccessfully to apply a policy of uniformly cutting loans to all customers, after careful consideration the bank eventually decided to put loan prioritization into practice as an emergency measure. The most important objective of this measure was to reduce the amount of loans to major borrowers whose main bank was not Mitsui Bank, or at worst to sever all business relations with them.

At the end of September 1953 the bank had 1059 major borrowers, each of whose outstanding debt to the bank amounted to more than 10 million yen (Table 4.5). About 14 300 companies whose outstanding debts to the bank were less than 10 million yen each were classified as small and medium-sized companies. The bank divided the 1059 major borrowers into two categories: companies whose main bank was Mitsui Bank (554) and companies whose main bank was not Mitsui Bank (505). The loans to these 1059 borrowers accounted for 86 per cent of the bank's total outstanding loans, and the total amount borrowed by the 554 main bank companies

Table 4.4 Mitsui Bank's fund position, 1952–53 (100 million yen)

Item	Balance at end September 1952	Increase/decrease			Total amount	Rate of increase
		Second half 1952	First half 1953	October–December 1953		
(a) Deposits	690	+169	+41	+66	+276	40.1
(b) Funds supplied	1070	+188	+104	+87	+379	35.5
Loans	896	+137	+119	+55	+311	34.7
Foreign exchange	99	+35	−40	+20	+15	15.5
Securities investment	75	+16	+25	+12	+53	71.1
Balance (a minus b)	−380	−19	−63	−21	−103	27.4
External barrowing	326	+22	+34	+30	+86	26.4
From the Bank of Japan	284	−7	+36	+20	+49	17.2
From the money market	42	+29	−2	+10	+37	87.7

Source: Mitsui Bank, 'Directives on Loan Screening from the 10th Branch Managers' Meeting', in 'Records of Mitsui Bank's Branch Managers' Meetings' (unpublished).

Table 4.5 Mitsui Bank's loan to deposit ratio, 1952–53 (100 million yen)

	Number of borrowers	End September 1952			End September 1953		
		Loans	Deposits	Loan to deposit ratio (%)	Loans	Deposits	Loan to deposit ratio (%)
Main bank Mitsui	554	571	146	25.5	732	173	23.6
Main bank other banks	505	188	74	39.3	258	111	43.0
A	313	144	56	38.8	194	89	45.8
B	192	44	18	40.9	64	22	34.3
Sub-total	1059	759	220	28.9	990	284	28.6
Small and medium sized companies	14 330	130	78	60.0	159	97	61.0
Total	14 884	889	298	33.5	1149	381	33.1

A means the companies exempted from loan cutting and B means the companies selected as targets for loan cutting.

Source: Mitsui Bank 'Directives on Loan Screening from the 10th Branch Managers' Meeting', in 'Records of Mitsui Bank's Branch Managers' Meetings' (unpublished).

outweighed that borrowed by the remaining 505 by a ratio of 74 to 12. The ratio of deposits held on behalf of the 554 companies to the outstanding loans to these companies was 23.6 per cent. This highly unsatisfactory situation was no doubt one of the most important reasons for the bank's serious fund shortage and therefore it should have selected some of these companies as the main targets of its loan prioritization. However it instead decided to cut down its loans to the 505 companies whose main bank was not Mitsui Bank, and to ask other financial institutions to share the burden of providing funds to the companies for whom it served as main bank. According to Table 4.6 overleaf other financial institutions were asked to share this burden in respect of 120 companies whose outstanding debt to the bank exceeded 100 million yen each, but it appears that its requests were scarcely realized. Though there were still 53 companies which appeared capable of doing so, their situation was in fact too pitiful to be able to do so. In addition, other financial institutions seemed not to share the burden of providing funds, disregarding the bank's will. The bank then selected 192 of the 505 major borrowers whose main banks were other than Mitsui as its main targets for loan cutting. Interestingly, 17 of the 84 prewar Mitsui-affiliated companies were included among those whose main bank was not Mitsui Bank, as Table 4.7 (p. 77) shows.[21]

Competitive pressure for loans

During the decade of high-speed economic growth (1955 onwards), Japanese banks engaged twice in intense lending competitions, once for the provision of loans to major companies during the boom that preceded the stubborn recession of 1958, and once after the recession for the provision of loans to promising small and medium-sized businesses and major companies. In general, during the former period they offered long-term capital loans from their own funds in order to win the competition, but after the recession, when they were forced to put loan prioritization into practice again, they had to ask other financial institutions to share the burden of such loans. Rolled over short-term loans were the most important form of long-term borrowing for major companies, but such stance of the banks prevented them from offering extensive long-term capital loans in the long run despite not being prohibited from doing so by law.

Table 4.6 Mitsui Bank's loans to 554 companies whose main bank was Mitsui Bank, September 1953 (100 million yen)

Companies whose outstanding debts to the bank were	Loans from the bank were	Number	Total loans	Total deposits	Balance
more than 100 million yen	Excessive	53	246	44	202
	Suitable	39	243	52	191
	Insufficient	9	50	22	28
	Considerably short	19	69	14	55
	Total	120	608	132	476
Companies whose outstanding debts to the bank were from 10 to 100 million yen		434	124	41	83
Total		554	732	173	559

Source: Mitsui Bank, 'Directives on Loan Screening from the 10th Branch Managers' Meeting', in 'Records of Mitsui Bank's Branch Managers' Meetings' (unpublished).

Table 4.7 Mitsui Bank's loans to 84 prewar Mitsui-affiliated companies, 1952–53 (100 million yen)

	End of September 1952		End of September 1953	
	Number	Outstanding loans	Number	Outstanding loans
Companies whose main bank was Mitsui Bank	67	346	69	411
Companies whose outstanding debts to the bank were more than 100 million yen	52	336	53	404
Companies whose outstanding debts to the bank were from 10 to 100 million yen	15	10	16	7
Companies whose main bank was not Mitsui Bank	17	10	17	14
Total (A)	84	356	86	425
The bank's total outstanding loans (B)		890		1149
A/B (%)		40.0		36.9

Source: Mitsui Bank, 'Directives on Loan Screening from the 10th Branch Managers' Meeting', in 'Records of Mitsui Bank's Branch Managers' Meetings' (unpublished).

Mitsui Bank, which was still experiencing a fund shortage problem, was among the banks that were most eager to ask other financial institutions to share the burden of providing long-term capital loans to major companies.

Most of the companies targeted by Mitsui and the other large banks belonged to or were connected with the heavy and chemical industries because the Japanese economy was shifting towards a heavy and chemical industries-oriented industrial structure.[22] According to the report on a Mitsui Bank branch managers' meeting, in January 1956, 1955 was an epoch-making year in financing, and banks rushed to provide loans at preferential interest rates to promising companies – eminent trading companies in particular – as soon as their loan–deposit imbalance was resolved. Mitsui Bank's deposits increased by 22 billion yen but its loan increase was only 600 million yen because of the loan prioritization it had introduced in 1954. The bank was able to pay off 18 600 million yen of its debt to the Bank of Japan, so its cash position improved rather rapidly, though its fund shortage problem was not completely resolved.[23]

The most interesting thing is how Mitsui Bank tried to win the intensifying lending competition under the circumstances that the strong got stronger and the weak got weaker among its customers with the shift in the industrial structure towards emphasis on the heavy and chemical industries. A clear answer can be found in the reports of branch managers' meetings held between January 1956 and January 1958. The report of the meeting in January 1956 states that:

> The crucial point is that we must improve our loan composition. In other words we must increase our loans to promising companies while helping companies whose business is poor to recover during this boom period. We must reduce our loans or ask other financial institutions to share the burden of providing loans to companies that are unlikely to recover or to be superior to fellow companies.[24]

The report of the August 1956 meeting shows that Japan's six largest banks – Mitsui, Mitsubishi, Sumitomo, Fuji, Sanwa and Dai-Ichi – were winning the lending competition:

> The most striking thing is that the race among banks to provide mainly long-term capital loans to promising companies has stimulated the latter to reduce the number of banks they deal with. We have now entered a new stage that is characterized by the selection of banks by borrowers. Japan's six largest banks are winning the lending competition, as might have been expected. Banks that have increased their loans by more than 10 billion yen are restricted to these six.[25]

According to the report of the January 1958 meeting the final winners of the competition were the former zaibatsu-affiliated banks: Mitsubishi, Sumitomo and Mitsui. There were three main factors that made these banks superior to the rest: an increase in their loans to the former zaibatsu-affiliated trading companies, their long-term loans to basic industries and their provision of inventory finance to large manufacturers at the start of the recession.[26]

By the end of the 1956–57 or so-called 'Jinmu' boom, the six largest banks had succeeded in establishing firmer relations with most of the promising major companies, the latter becoming the most important priority borrowers for each of them. Thereafter the loan composition of these banks came to resemble each other, and the differences between the loan compositions of the former zaibatsu-affiliated banks and those of the rest almost disappeared.

It seems that the banks increased their long-term loans to an excessive degree during the lending competition:

> Banks have become careless enough to provide long-term capital loans to their customers in excess of the limits allowed to them as commercial banks. Mitsui Bank's percentage of outstanding long-term capital loans to total outstanding loans was 7.71 per cent at the end of March 1956, rather higher than the 5.54 per cent average for the other major banks. Though this was to some extent unavoidable as it had a lot of major companies as customers, it is quite important to ask other specialist financial institutions such as the Industrial Bank of Japan and the Long-Term Credit Bank of Japan to share the burden of providing these loans.[27]

As Tables 4.8 and 4.9 show, the share of outstanding long-term capital loans in total outstanding loans at Mitsui was higher than that of the other large banks at the end of March 1956, and it peaked at 12.7 per cent at the end of 1958. Such a rise in the share during the years 1956–58 got a fairly long average loan period, though the share of long-term capital loans in total outstanding loans at Mitsui at the end of 1958 was considerably below what it had been at the end of 1937 (20.6 per cent. The bank's average loan period had been 1.63 months in the second half 1937 and 1.72 months in the first half of 1938). The bank's average loan period in 1957 was considerably longer than two months.

Between the end of September 1955 and the end of March 1957 the share of outstanding loans with a loan period of two months or less in Mitsui's total outstanding loans decreased and the share of loans with a loan period of more than twelve months increased considerably, while the average percentages for 13 other large banks (shown in parentheses) changed only slightly during this period and the proportion of short-term loans remained high:

- Two months or less: fell from 33.8 per cent to 31.7 per cent (fell from 46.3 per cent to 43.0 per cent).

Table 4.8 Outstanding long-term loans, Japan's six largest banks, 1956–57 (100 million yen)

	End March 1956		End September 1956		End March 1957		Increase during 6 months from the end March 1956		Increase during 6 months from the end September 1956	
	Amount	(%)*	Amount	(%)*	Amount	(%)*	Amount	Rate of increase (%)	Amount	Rate of increase (%)
Mitsui	109	7.5	143	8.5	185	9.6	34	31.2	42	29.4
Daiichi	86	5.7	107	6.0	145	7.0	21	24.4	38	32.5
Fuji	147	6.4	181	6.7	229	7.2	34	23.1	48	26.5
Mitsubishi	159	7.2	199	7.8	248	8.2	40	25.2	49	24.6
Sumitomo	95	4.6	123	5.0	197	6.8	28	29.5	74	60.1
Sanwa	73	3.3	99	3.8	131	4.3	26	35.6	32	32.3

*Percentage of total outstanding loans.

Source: Mitsui Bank, 'Directives on Loan Screening from the 17th Branch Managers' Meeting', in 'Records of Mitsui Bank's Branch Manager's Meetings' (unpublished).

Table 4.9 Outstanding long-term loans, 13 largest commercial banks, 1956–59 (100 million yen)

	Mitsui		Other 12 banks (average)	
	Amount	*(%)**	*Amount*	*(%)**
End December 1956	159	8.9	112	6.0
End March 1957	185	9.6	127	6.4
End June 1957	212	10.3	143	6.9
End September 1957	246	11.2	162	7.4
End December 1957	281	12.1	177	7.6
End March 1958	294	12.4	185	7.7
End June 1958	306	12.6	193	7.9
End September 1958	311	12.5	199	7.9
End December 1958	333	12.7	208	7.9
End March 1959	334	12.5	211	7.9
End June 1959	321	11.7	215	7.8
End September 1959	318	11.1	221	7.7
End December 1959	316	10.4	227	7.4

*Percentage of total outstanding loans.

Sources: Mitsui Bank, 'Directives on Loan Screening from the 19th Branch Managers' Meeting' and 'Directives on Loan Screening from the 22nd Branch Managers' Meeting', in 'Records of Mitsui Bank's Managers' Meetings' (unpublished).

- Two to three months: rose from 24.7 per cent to 26.2 per cent (rose from 30.9 per cent to 33.4 per cent).
- Three to twelve months: fell from 31.8 per cent to 28.4 per cent (rose from 16.5 per cent to 16.8 per cent).
- Over twelve months: rose from 9.3 per cent to 11.5 per cent (fell from 5.4 per cent to 5.2 per cent).
- Overdrafts: rose from 0.2 per cent to 2.0 per cent (rose from 0.6 per cent to 1.4 per cent).

When the government introduced tight monetary policy at the time of the 1958 recession, banks relapsed into quite unfavourable fund positions. In order to avoid the use of loan prioritization some of these banks eventually decided to ask other financial institutions, such as long-term credit banks and government financial institutions, to share the burden of providing long-term loans to major companies instead of establishing their own long-term lending business. This shows that they had come to accept the existence and role of the specialist financial institutions that had been established when the country's financial system had been reorganized.

The Development Bank of Japan and the Export–Import Bank of Japan had been established as government financial institutions in 1951. In 1952, under the Law for Long-Term Credit Banks, the Long-Term Credit Bank of Japan had been founded and the Industrial Bank of Japan had reverted from being a deposit bank (previously the IBJ had become a commercial bank under SCAP's policy of forcing certain banks – including Nippon Kangyo Bank, Hokkaido Takushoku Bank and Yokohama Specie Bank – to become commercial banks that also engaged in bond issuing). Finally, from 1952 trust banks had been entitled to conduct long-term lending business under the Loan Trust Law.[28]

Mitsui Bank was the first of the six largest banks to ask other financial institutions to share the burden of providing long-term capital loans to companies with which it had formed firm ties through loan relationships during the 1954 recession and the 1956–57 boom. When doing so it was necessary to strengthen the defensive wall around its core affiliated companies in order to prevent the probable spread of influence by the financial institutions upon which it depended. That seems to be the reason why the 'Second Thursday Club' (*Nimokukai*), a meeting of the chairmen and presidents of all 18 companies comprising the Mitsui group, was formed during the final phase of the 1959–61 'Iwado' boom, when the bank again became involved in a heated lending competition with the other large banks.[29]

The reinforcement of affiliated groups through loan relationships and cross-shareholdings were the most striking features of the lending competition during the 1959–61. Keeping this in mind, we shall describe how Mitsui Bank tried to win the lending competition.

Although Mitsui Bank succeeded in increasing its loans to promising major companies in the lending competition during the 1956–57 boom, it lagged behind the rest of the six largest banks, except Dai-Ichi Bank, both in the provision of loans to small and medium-sized businesses and in developing its business as a foreign exchange bank. Such operations were to some extent sacrificed during the periods of selective lending and loan prioritization (which were more strict than those of other banks) in the 1954 and 1958 recessions. Even during the 1956–57 boom the amount of funds allocated by the bank to these businesses was relatively small.

The bank was provided with a good opportunity to develop these activities after 1958 when Daiichi Bussan merged with Muromachi Bussan, which led to the reestablishment of Mitsui and Company in February the following year. However this opportunity was not fully exploited because the emphasis of the six largest banks during the lending competition that took place in the 1959–61 boom shifted to promising major companies in the heavy and chemical industries.

During the 1958 recession the bank turned its attention to providing loans to promising trading companies in order to develop its foreign exchange business. At that time the government was strongly pushing its export promotion policy, aimed at building an export-led economy, and the disparity between the degrees of expertise of the foreign exchange banks was becoming more obvious. The bank's principal aim during this period was to secure a 10 per cent market share of the nation's foreign exchange business, and to this end it targeted non-affiliated trading companies as well as affiliated ones. Among the affiliated companies it managed to secure the majority of Mitsui and Company's foreign exchange transactions. Predicting correctly that without close cooperation with the general trading companies, both major manufacturers and expert foreign exchange banks could not take risks contained in large scale profitable undertakings, the bank concluded that the superiority of general trading companies over major manufacturers and other trade-related businesses would soon become obvious.[30]

Until the 1960s general trading companies – including Mitsui and Company – acted more in the manner of commission merchants by avoiding or spreading risk as much as possible, but in the 1960s they began to handle a wide range of merchandise according to a basic risk-reduction strategy. As a result they were able to impress upon major manufacturers their strong fund-raising capabilities and ability to handle the importation of important raw materials and the exportation of manufactured products, and to make the banks aware of their expert product knowledge.[31] Mitsui Bank's foreign exchange transactions with general and specialized trading companies accounted for around 40 per cent of its total foreign exchange transactions at the end of the 1950s (Table 4.10). However its overall market share slumped, reflecting a heated competition among banks to provide loans to prominent general trading companies, both affiliated and non-affiliated.

Table 4.10   Mitsui Bank's foreign exchange transactions, April–December 1959 ($ million)

	April–September 1959		October–December 1959	
	Amount	(%)	Amount	(%)
Affiliated general trading companies (5)	94.1	32.0	57.8	31.4
Non-affiliated general trading companies (4)	7.9	2.7	5.7	3.1
Specialized trading companies (8)	15.7	5.3	10.0	5.4
Oil companies (5)	23.3	7.9	13.4	7.3
Manufacturers (4)	15.1	5.1	13.7	7.5
Shipping companies (2)	7.6	2.6	4.2	2.3
Electric power companies (2)	2.3	0.8	1.7	0.9
Others	128.5	43.6	77.3	42.1
Total	294.5	100.0	183.8	100.0

Source: Mitsui Bank, 'Directives on Foreign Exchange Operations from the 22nd Branch Managers' Meeting', in 'Records of Mitsui Bank's Branch Managers' Meetings' (unpublished).

Another feature of this lending competition was that the six largest banks began to pay more attention to small and medium-sized businesses. At the end of 1957 Mitsui Bank had lagged far behind the other large banks in the provision of loans to small and medium-sized businesses, but after an examination by the Bank of Japan in 1958 it began to increase its loans to such businesses using funds it had saved by persuading other financial institutions to share the burden of providing long-term capital loans to major companies. An interesting aspect of this policy shift is that it was accompanied by a change in the criteria used to choose major companies as customers. The new targets were companies in industries that had many allied industries and subcontractors as well as a great potential for growth. In this it followed the economy's shift towards the heavy and chemical industries, and succeeded in cropping fruit such as Toshiba and Toyota Motors.[32]

Summary

In postwar Japan the banking sector recovered somewhat more rapidly than other sectors and the major banks were essentially back on their feet by the autumn of 1948. Between 1948 and the start of the 1950s the former zaibatsu-affiliated banks began to act as the main banks for major companies that had belonged to the zaibatsu. Mitsui Bank took a similar course of action, but lost half of its branch network and half of its funds when it was separated from Dai-Ichi Bank as a result of Teikoku Bank's dissolution.

Fuji Bank came to dominate the other major banks after engaging in an aggressive strategy to increase its share of trading financing. The other banks strove desperately to catch up, and lending competitions became an ongoing characteristic of the banking sector.

In July 1947 Mitsui and Company was broken up into more than 200 separate companies, the most prominent of which were Daiichi Trading and Daiichi Bussan. Mitsui Bank did not rate Daiichi Bussan as highly as Daiichi Trading until about 1951, which is why it asked Fuji Bank to share the burden of providing funds to Daiichi Bussan while maintains a close relationship with the company as its main bank. Thus Fuji Bank became Daiichi Bussan's main creditor and would have also become its main bank if general panic had not gripped the trading companies and countermeasures had not been taken against it by Mitsui Bank.

By 1954 Mitsui Bank had regained its position as the main creditor of Daiichi Bussan, which was trying to retrieve the name 'Mitsui and Company'. This might have meant that Mitsui Bank would increase its loans and regain its position as the main creditor of former affiliates, which had reluctantly transferred to other banks. On the contrary, however the bank asked other financial institutions to share the burden of loan provision, particularly long-term capital loans to the previously affiliated companies with which it had formed ties through loan relationships during the 1954 recession and the 1956–57 boom. When doing so the bank considered it prudent to strengthen the defensive wall around its core of affiliated companies against the probable spread of influence by the financial institutions upon which it depended.

5
Supplementary Devices to Win the Lending Battle, 1961–65

During the early 1960s Mitsui Bank continued to balance the foundations of its business and form firmer ties with companies without offering extensive long-term capital loans and a full securities service. Then the bank organized cross-shareholdings and scheduled regular meetings between the bank and the presidents of its major customers in the hope that this would increase its dealings between its major trading customers, particularly Mitsui and Company, and important customers in the heavy and chemical industries, and that such transactions would help it to maintain its high ratio of loans to wholesalers (mainly major trading companies) to total outstanding loans. These meetings and cross-shareholdings were also seen as a way to ensure that it would remain the main bank of these customers. The bank became more cautious about asking other financial institutions to share the burden of providing loans to its customers as the loan competition among the major commercial banks and between these banks and the IBJ became intense.

I would like to pause here for a word about the material upon which Chapters 5 and 6 are based. During the research for this book, for the pre-World War II period I was fortunate to gain access to documents unavailable to the general public in addition to published documents and books, but gaining access to confidential documents post-dating World War II was much more difficult because many remain sensitive. I was able to use reports on Mitsui Bank's branch managers' meetings – still unavailable to the public – to describe the lending activities of the bank and its competitors prior to 1960, but thereafter this text is based purely on publicly available sources. The latter – including bank's histories, published to commemorate anniversaries – while helpful, fail to mention several important problems: they do not refer to the difficulties caused by tightened reserve positions or shortages of funds – more specifically, they do not reveal the fact that Japan's largest commercial banks had to give up their plans to expand their long-term loan business because they faced fund shortage problems; and they seldom refer to their bad debt problems, their lending policy for each individual customers, the real nature of the relationship between them and their customers, their individual lobbying activities and so on.

Bearing these limitations in mind, we shall now examine the kinds of supplementary device that banks introduced to intensify their unification with business groups.

Fund shortages

In general, after the postwar reconstruction period, for a decade plant and equipment investment was mainly responsible for economic growth. With this investment boom the demand for long-term capital loans increased rapidly, and consequently it became imperative for banks to acquire a great amount of funds. As stated earlier, at the beginning of the 1950s the former zaibatsu-affiliated banks tended to act as the nucleus for enterprises that had once belonged to the zaibatsu. This tendency became even stronger in the mid 1950s, when Japan's high-speed economic growth started, and the other major banks began to follow suit.

Large enterprises obtained huge financial support from the banks and actively engaged in the expansion of their traditional undertakings. At the same time they diversified into new areas, where they competed vigorously for market share. Enterprises that operated in different areas but had financial links tended to group together for closer cooperation.

As a result of the extensive financial support given by the banks to the enterprises, the former's excess loan situation worsened despite fact that relaxation of the regulations governing the opening of new branch offices was helping them to attract deposits.[1] Some might wonder why the fund shortage problem continued for banks and enterprises alike in the 1960s, since the economy obviously had enough funds to make its high-speed growth possible. However the wartime experience shows that the Japanese economy was able to grow despite bank fund shortages, and it seems that this held true even in peaceful times. As before, the shortage was resolved by excessive borrowing from the Bank of Japan.

According to the official history of Mitsui Bank, the major banks' excess loan situation intensified after the mid 1950s because the rapid increase in the scale of corporate operations was not backed by accumulated capital and companies had to borrow considerable amounts. On the other hand, personal savings rose in line with rises in the national income level and the savings rate remained high throughout the period of high-speed economic growth. As a result the share in total personal financial assets of time deposits in banks rose substantially. However the major banks were still not able to attract enough deposits to meet the enterprises' demand for funds. Their ratio of loans to deposits increased by more than 100 per cent between 1957 and 1964, necessitating increased borrowing from the Bank of Japan and other financial institutions.

To curtail borrowing by the major banks, prior to 1963 the Bank of Japan placed considerable emphasis on the control of bank lending, but thereafter its policy emphasis changed to reliance on such market mechanisms as interest rate fluctuations and adjustments to banks' reserve to deposit ratios.

The Ministry of Finance had begun to take action to resolve the banks' excess loan situation in 1961, when the Ministry's Financial System Research Council (*Kinyu Seido Chosakai*) had established a division to look into the problem. After two-years of research the division presented its proposals, but the Federated Bankers Association of Japan (*Zenkoku Ginko Kyokai Rengokai*) responded negatively to these proposals, and submitted a revised version to the ministry. Faced with such strong opposition the ministry was forced to abandon its effort in August 1963.[2] As will be discussed later, the Ministry of International Trade and Industry also attempted to interfere in the affairs of private banks in order to gain financial backing for its industrial policy.

The purpose of the presidents' meetings

The regular meetings of the presidents of banks and customer companies and cross-shareholdings among these companies were set up as devices to strengthen the unification of business groups, with major banks as their nuclei, and were an inevitable consequence of the large banks' decision to ask other financial institutions to share the burden of loan provision.

As noted earlier, the six largest banks had formed firm ties with major and promising companies by the recession of 1958, after which they had had to ask other financial institutions, particularly long-term credit institutions, to share the burden of providing extra loans to maintain these ties and ensure success in the lending competition. This in turn meant that they were forced to introduce measures to protect their status as main bank and to take precautions against the competition for custom that was expected to arise from the burden sharing. It should be pointed out that these precautions were not aimed at preventing these institutions from poaching their customers as this would have been practically impossible after the mid 1950s. Rather they were aimed at preventing the institutions from viewing transactions with the banks' customers as a vested right.

The business groups that resulted from the frequent meetings of presidents and cross-shareholdings became the essence of the so-called new main bank system. As the latter was considered to be a consequence of the serious fund shortage problem it was initially regarded as temporary, and it was assumed that the normal relationships between main banks and their major customers would resume after the resolution of the problem.

The establishment of business groups

This section examines the business groups associated with Mitsui Bank, Fuji Bank and Sanwa Bank. We shall also examine the activities of the IBJ, which shared with the commercial banks the burden of providing loans to companies. By putting together the accounts published by these banks we can gain a clearer picture of the nature of the business groups, although these accounts fail to mention why the groups were formed and the part played in this by the banks' fund shortage problem.

According to the official history of Mitsui Bank, regular meetings between representatives of the Mitsui affiliates took place spontaneously. The 'Monday Club' was formed in 1950 and its membership consisted of executive directors or higher-ranking officers of

20 Mitsui affiliates. Despite their regular meetings, however, the members of the Monday Club never planned group actions. The 'Second Thursday Club' – meetings of the chairmen and presidents of all 18 corporations that comprised the Mitsui group – was launched in 1961 and developed into a forum for discussing matters common to the group and plans for new undertakings.

The formation of the Mitsui group took place much later than that of the Mitsubishi and Sumitomo groups, ostensibly because the bank could not conduct its business as a member of the 'old established firm of Mitsui', and because it wished to avoid business group involvement during the postwar period when the economy was being democratized. However the bank's official history contradicts itself in that it states elsewhere that the main reasons for the delay were that Mitsui Bank, the central financial institution for the Mitsui affiliates, had insufficient funds to lend them because it had only a small number of branches to which to attract depositors, and that the companies in the Mitsui group needed more time than other companies to reconstruct themselves because Mitsui had been SCAP's main target in the zaibatsu dissolution.[3]

Turning now to Fuji Bank, in the late 1950s the bank's customers became eager to cooperate with one another in the development of nuclear power as a source of energy and to participate in the petro-chemical industry. In response, in July 1959 the bank established a section in the loan application department to attend to these customers' borrowing requirements. The section's main role was to liaise with the priority borrowers, and before long it was organizing regular meetings between the presidents of the companies in question. At that stage the bank's executive office and planning office took over its duties, and in January 1966 they established the 'Fuyo [Confederate Rose] Group'. The resultant meetings between the presidents of the group companies were not intended as a forum for group decision making but to ensure the regular exchange of opinions and information within the group. The original group had 25 members, including Fuji Bank.[4]

According to the bank's official history the main reason for establishing the Fuyo Group was to cement ties with companies in the face of competition from the former zaibatsu-affiliated banks. Interestingly, in the early 1960s Fuji Bank was one of the more aggressive of the six largest banks. While most banks with a severe fund shortage problem asked other financial institutions to share the burden of extending loans to their customers, Fuji Bank alone shouldered the burden of providing short-term loans to its customers while the IBJ took on the task of providing mainly long-term loans.

Sanwa Bank's official history gives us the best idea of which banks took the lead in establishing presidential meetings (or meetings of chairmen and presidents) among their top priority borrowers during the late 1950s and early 1960s, and why. One of the most remarkable banking developments of the following decade was the expansion by the large banks of loans to their affiliated companies. This was particularly true of the former zaibatsu-affiliated banks. It is claimed in Sanwa Bank's history that some of its customers joined groups connected with the former zaibatsu-affiliated banks when companies previously affiliated with zaibatsu tried to take over companies geared to Japan's structural shift towards investment in technology. Taking the offensive by the former zaibatsu-affiliated banks into account, it was important for Sanwa Bank to build a corporate network as well as to boost transactions with individual customers when it decided to prioritize loans to the heavy and chemical industries.[5]

To strengthen its corporate network, in 1957 the bank carried out an organizational reform of its loan application department. In order to deal with its major customers' needs more comprehensively, one department was devoted exclusively to the examination of loan applications by these customers. In 1960 the bank established a councillor's office to deal with corporate affairs. Its immediate tasks were to help with the development of two petrochemical complexes in the Chiba and Sakai coastal industrial zones and to create stronger bonds with the Hitachi group. Regular meetings of the chairmen and presidents of the 23 companies comprising the Sanwa Group, called the 'Third Wednesday Group' (*Sansuikai*) began in 1967.[6]

The Industrial Bank of Japan and its rivalry with the commercial banks

Under the terms of the Law for Long-Term Credit Banks of December 1952 the IBJ was reorganized into a private bank specializing in long-term capital lending. The bank followed the strategy adopted by the six largest commercial banks, which in the mid 1950s had begun to group together the largest and most promising of their customers. In this way the IBJ became a rival of the commercial banks. By the early 1960s it had grouped some of its major customers around it as the main bank, while at the same time continuing to provide customers of the commercial banks with long-term capital loans, as before.

Although the bank did not establish meetings of the presidents of its major customers it took other measures analogous to such meetings in order to strengthen its links with these companies and win the lending competition. To set up regular meetings of affiliated companies' presidents would have been meaningless for the bank as it already thought of itself as the main bank of almost all Japan's major companies in respect of long-term capital lending. The bank's measures were mainly aimed at taking the lead in reorganizing the major industries and cutting their capital expenditure programmes and demand for long-term loans. This was done in cooperation with government departments in charge of financial and industrial policies.

In much the same way as the large commercial banks, the IBJ experienced a fund shortage problem and was forced to introduce loan prioritization. It also asked commercial banks to share the burden of providing loans to shipping companies. From 1955, when monetary conditions eased, the bank joined in the lending competition and succeeded in forming firmer ties with such promising large companies as Nissan Motors and Hitachi, while sharing its lending to non-affiliated companies with the latter's main banks.[7]

After 1957, when the government began to pursue a tight monetary policy, the IBJ eventually succeeded in adapting its loan composition to the structural shift towards the heavy and chemical industries. However its share of the total long-term loans provided by financial institutions decreased and its fund shortage problem became more serious because the largest commercial banks decided not to increase their long-term loans to the heavy and chemical industries but to ask other credit institutions for help with long-term loan provision.

The bank's loans to the chemical, oil refining, steel, nonferrous metals and machinery industries rose from 25.2 per cent of its total outstanding loans at the end of March 1956 to 40.3 per cent at the end of March 1961. In particular, loans to the steel, machinery and chemical industries accounted for 13.4 per cent, 11.5 per cent and 11.6 per cent respectively of total outstanding loans at the end of March 1961 and constituted, together with its loans to the electric power industry, the most important part of its lending. Two other long-term credit banks and the trust banks had achieved almost the same loan composition as the IBJ by the beginning of the 1960s.[8]

The crucial point here is that the IBJ succeeded in attaining a healthy loan composition without establishing presidential meetings and cross-shareholdings. Conversely the six largest commercial banks might not have succeeded in achieving beneficial long-term loan compositions (because of their fund shortage problem) in the absence of such meetings and cross-shareholding.

Like the IBJ, in the late 1950s the large commercial banks expanded their loans to manufacturing industries, particularly to enterprises in the heavy and chemical sectors. Such loans rose to 44 per cent of total outstanding loans, compared with 56 per cent in the case of three long-term credit banks. The commercial banks also extended loans indirectly through the purchase of debentures issued by the long-term credit banks to raise funds, stepping up their subscription to these debentures by 215.9 billion yen (compared with an increase in long-term loans of 291.5 billion yen) and boosting the credit banks' long-term loans by 34 per cent. They also increased their subscription to the IBJ's debentures by 95 billion yen (2.7 times more than in the early 1950s), thus contributing to a 31 per cent surge in the bank's outstanding long-term loans.[9]

The IBJ was forced to take stronger measures to resolve its fund shortage problem after 1957, including, asking other financial institutions – such as local banks, life and non-life insurance companies and foreign financial institutions – to share the burden of making loans to its customers, while at the same time trying to raise more funds by asking commercial banks to subscribe to its debentures, as noted above.[10] Furthermore it acted to adjust the supply and demand of long-term loans. More specifically, it reduced or postponed loans to major companies for whom it served as the main bank in respect of long-term loans.

In July 1957 the Financial Institutions Fund Council, established in 1956 as an advisory organ of the Minister of Finance, set up a special committee to find a way of cutting plant and equipment investment. The IBJ's president, Teiichi Kawakita, joined the committee as one of several representatives from financial circles. In the same year the Federated Bankers Association of Japan established a fund adjustment committee (*shikin chosei iinkai*) to persuade banks voluntarily to adjust the amount of their loans, and the Industrial Rationalization Commission (*Sangyo Gorika Shingikai*), an advisory body for the minister of international trade and industry, created a fund section (*shikin bukai*) to reduce plant and equipment investment by adjusting bank loans for such investment. The IBJ's vice-president, Sohei Nakayama (an influential leader of the Japanese Association of Corporate Executives and responsible for the bank's success in forming firmer ties with major companies), joined the fund section as a representative of the bank.[11]

During the prosperous years of 1959–61 the lending competition among Japan's largest banks stepped up. As noted earlier, in order to win the competition Mitsui Bank asked other financial institutions to share the burden of providing long-term loans to its customers, but Fuji Bank and others that had not yet properly forged their corporate groupings continued to increase their provision of both long-term and short-term loans to their customers in order to entice these customers in their groups.

Fuji Bank's main targets were companies formerly affiliated with the Nissan zaibatsu, such as Nissan Motors, and Hitachi. Hitachi and Nissan Motors had been the most important companies in the Nissan zaibatsu in the interwar years, but the unity among the zaibatsu companies had begun to weaken during World War II and just after the war the zaibatsu had been dissolved. However in the 1950s the previously affiliated companies had gradually started to reunite by establishing cross-shareholdings and excluding competitors from participating in their group dealings. Although the new group's unity was not overly strong, it included many major or promising companies in the heavy and chemical industries.[12] In General most of the companies targeted by Fuji Bank were also important customers of the IBJ.

The intense lending competition, particularly in respect of the IBJ's major customers, caused a severe fund shortage problem for the banks concerned, and it was this that triggered the government's tight monetary policy after 1962.

By early 1962 the IBJ's fund position had deteriorated markedly and its external debt approached 40 billion yen, the limit allowed to it. The previous year the bank had asked other financial institutions to share the burden of providing loans to its major borrowers, and as a result the bank's share of the total long-term loans provided to them fell sharply from 25.1 per cent to 14.7 per cent between March 1961 and March 1962 while those of the largest commercial banks, life and non-life insurance companies, The Development Bank of Japan and foreign financial institutions rose strikingly. The IBJ's official history notes somewhat ironically: 'In particular, the largest commercial banks expanded their long-term loans to their affiliated companies, even though they were faced with bad fund positions.'[13]

In 1962, the IBJ, as a private bank, was forced to implement a loan prioritization programme to resolve its fund shortage, much as most of Japan's largest commercial banks had had to do during the recession of 1954. The steel, automotive and electrical machinery industries were given first priority as borrowers. The bank put particular emphasis on a small number of leading companies, such as Yawata Steel, Fuji Steel, Nissan Motors and Hitachi, companies that were also the main long-term loan targets of some of the large commercial banks.

At this point the IBJ was requested by the government to take the lead, in cooperation with the leading financial institutions, in persuading private industrial companies to reduce their investment in plant and equipment. The bank held the same opinion as the government with regard to the adoption of an industrial policy for the reorganization of industries and the strengthening of their international competitiveness. They were agreed on the need for the bank to put loan prioritization into effect and comply actively with the industrial policy.

The automotive industry became the bank's first target for two reasons. The first was because this industry, together with the petrochemical industry, was continuing to increase its investment in plant and equipment in order to strengthen its international competitiveness, despite the government's tight monetary policy. The second was because Nissan Motors, a customer of the IBJ, was pleased to increase investment in plant and equipment.[14]

In light of Nissan Motors' leading position among its group at the beginning of the 1960s, to succeed in becoming the main bank meant strengthening the group's ties. To this end Fuji Bank was urged by the government to establish meetings of presidents, cross-shareholdings and so on, and to establish the best possible loan composition on the basis of affiliated companies and reflecting the structural shift towards the heavy and chemical industries. The IBJ was also urged to firm its ties with the group to reflect the increase in long-term loans to these industries.

Industrial policy and MITI

Mitsui Bank's practice of asking other financial institutions to share the burden of providing long-term loans to major companies was more or less true of the rest of Japan's six largest banks after the 1958 recession. After the Ministry of Finance established a system of financial institutions specializing in long-term lending – government financial institutions, long-term credit banks and trust banks – the government's next task was to formulate a suitable policy to smooth the provision of funds by these institutions to major companies. The Ministry of International Trade and Industry (MITI) accordingly tabled a provisional law for the promotion of specified industries (tokutei sangyo shinko rinji sochi ho), which from a financial point of view was quite similar to the wartime system of obliging banks to make preferential loans to companies designated as important to the war effort. The bill was presented to the Diet in 1963 and again in 1964, but failed to pass because of the private sector's strong opposition to the implied economic control by bureaucrats. Nonetheless cofinancing by commercial banks and financial institutions specializing in long-term lending was increasingly used to increase the total amount available to major companies for investment in new plant and equipment during the period of high-speed growth.

Needless to say, MITI had its own reasons for fostering strategic industries (the automotive, steel, heavy and electrical machinery, and petrochemical industries). For example MITI had been interested in fostering the automotive industry since immediately after World War II, but its main drive came when the industry was identified in the 1960s as strategically important to exports under Prime Minister Hayato Ikeda's 'national income doubling plan'. Prior to this the 1956 Provisional Law for the Promotion of the Machinery Industry (*Kikai Kogyo Shiko Rinji Sochi Ho*) had enabled car parts manufacturers to acquire low-interest financing to renovate their facilities.

MITI was well aware of the structural defects of the Japanese machinery industry. First, the industry did not have the capacity to support by itself the development of the automotive industry, and if the automotive industry did not develop, the related industrial machinery sector would not develop either. Second, the machinery industry relied too heavily on the in-house manufacture of parts, materials and machines. Finally, the industry was too dependent on the domestic market.

These structural defects were first pointed out by Takuji Komiyama in *Nihon Chusho Kogyo Kenkyu* (A Study of Small and Medium-Sized Industries in Japan, 1941), which subsequently became a bible for researchers on the subject. First, at the beginning of World War II, when Komiyama wrote the book, Japanese machinery manufacturers were engaged in integrated production – that is, they produced their own parts rather than purchasing them from outside, – because the domestic conditions required for the development of a supply industry were absent and the industry enjoyed government protection. Large factories producing cars, aircraft and the like all relied on integrated production.

Second, some of these factories even produced their own raw materials, which should have been left to specialist companies. Also, they placed one kind of machine-tool which would be used only for a few months in order to make the annual supply of all parts used, and while also placing another kind of machine-tool which would not be able to satisfy the demand, even if it was fully operated. Such an imbalance badly impaired their efficiency and put them in an extremely unfavourable position in respect of depreciation and cost accounting.

Finally, car manufacturers such as Toyota not only had to establish their own steel works and machine-tool factories, they also had to acquire the technology and skills required to forge and cast parts such as cranks and gears and the relevant know-how was not readily available.[15]

Returning to MITI, the latter emphasized the advantage of three economies of scale as a principle for fostering the machinery industry: economies of scale of production, economies of scale through company integration and economies of scale arising from the combining of companies or groups of companies. 'It is disadvantageous to economies of scale of production for final assemblers to make their parts themselves, even if it is advantageous from the point of view of economies of scale of company integration.'[16] This was a very important criterion used by MITI to evaluate the efficiency of the industry. In short, MITI regarded excessive in-house production by major manufacturers and assemblers as one of the most serious defects of the machinery industry and stressed that the industry must be based on specialization rather than integration. One way of approaching this was to establish a close relationship between machinery manufacturers and general trading companies. This would kill two birds with one stone as most trading companies had been seriously damaged by the 1951 recession and were keen to expand into domestic and foreign trade in machines, and MITI wished to support them as much as it could in order to broaden Japan's export trade.

According to Shintaro Hayashi (1961) there were two production models in the Japanese machinery industry. The first was that the degree of dependence on export trade was so high that specialization between assemblers and parts manufacturers was well established, the latter had become both independent of assemblers and specialist producers, the cost of parts had fallen and the final products had become internationally competitive. The second was that the degree of dependence on export trade was not high and as a result specialization between assemblers and parts manufacturers was not so well established, the latter remained dependent on assemblers, the cost of parts was falling only slowly and the final products were less internationally competitive.[17]

Given this it is easy to understand why MITI was keen to foster the highly export-oriented sections of the machinery industry. In his book Hayashi pays special attention to the British and Swedish automotive industries.[18] In these countries he found a viable model for the development of export-oriented car production to compete in the US market. European car manufacturers, including those of Britain and Sweden, were rushing to enter the US market, but Hayashi argued that their Japanese counterparts would not be able to do likewise unless the industry eliminated its structural defects. Towards this end MITI first supported the establishment of large-scale enterprises specializing in parts assembly. It explained its objectives as follows:

Judging from the present supply and demand conditions it is desirable for … large-scale parts makers specializing in assembled parts to be created, while other parts makers ... specialize in basic parts.

In order to realize this it is important for parts makers producing the same kind of parts to cooperate and adjust their respective field of specialization, and in some cases to prepare for a tie-up or merger.

In addition, the final assemblers that use these parts should give parts makers technical guidance and assistance, plan and organize their orders better to concentrate on a small number of parts makers, and promote the standardization and simplification of parts.[19]

MITI supplied the producers of assembled parts with public sector funds on condition that they met its requirement for plant investment (see below).

Second, MITI required car producers to withdraw from the production of all parts except engines by raising their outsourcing rate. It was not difficult for them to comply with this requirement because it was accompanied by the appearance of large-scale parts assemblers. According to a white paper on small and medium-sized enterprises the outsourcing rate duly rose from under 50 per cent in the late 1950s to over 70 per cent in the late 1970s. More precisely, in 1978 the outsourcing rate of Japanese 'Company A' (presumably Toyota) was 75 per cent while that of US 'Company B' (presumably General Motors) was 52 per cent. Hence it seems that the outsourcing rate of Japanese car producers had easily surpassed that of their foreign counterparts by about 1970.[20]

Finally, MITI supplied automotive companies with public funds on condition that they increased their investment in plant, restrained or reduced the range of models made and promoted cooperation among manufacturers. It also urged manufacturers to strive to export a considerable number of mass-produced cars or to take advantage of mass production in general, and to comply with the law that prohibited excessive competition with one another and new entry into the industry.[21]

Commercial banks' attitude towards MITI's industrial policy

This section looks at why the large commercial banks allowed MITI to intervene in the affairs of their customers in the automotive industry. To do so it is necessary to return to the early 1930s – that is, around the time of Showa depression – because it was in that period that the industrial policy of MITI was born and the interesting relationship between MITI and the large banks began.

During the depression MITI introduced its industrial rationalization programme to resolve the problems that had arisen as a result of the financial panic of 1927, when the Matsukata-affiliated and the Kuhara-affiliated groups had gone bankrupt (the Matsukatas were a distinguished family from Satsuma [Kagoshima] and the Kuharas were a branch of the Fujita family from Choshu (Yamaguchi) and influential merchants with government connections). Following their bankruptcy the problem arose of how the Ministry of Commerce and Industry should help Kawasaki Shipbuilding and Jugo Bank (Matsukata) and Hitachi (Kuhara).

In 1930–31, the ministry asked a number of large banks to provide money for the large-scale merger operations alluded to earlier, whereby almost all the main shipbuilding companies would merge into one company and the four large electrical machinery companies would do likewise. Two prominent trading companies were to have played an important part in these operations, the principal of which was Mitsubishi. Mitsubishi-affiliated companies, including Hitachi (a relative of the owner family was a leader of Mitsubishi), were supposed to become the largest shareholders, or at least the most influential group in these two companies. But it soon became clear that the Mitsubishi-affiliated companies would not take part as far as the merged electrical machinery company was concerned. Although it is not clear whether or not Mitsubishi Bank wanted to support these projects, it is quite clear that Mitsubishi Shipbuilding, which was the parent company of Mitsubishi Electric, opposed the electrical machinery merger and in the end both projects collapsed.[22]

The ministry learned some important lessons from this failure. First, it realized that it was incredibly difficult to make the companies belonging to different zaibatsu groups harmonize. It would have to formulate a policy to promote production based on specialization, and a new policy for merger projects. Second, it learned that cooperation between the banks closely connected with the companies concerned was essential if its policies were to succeed. The ministry and its successors seem to have drawn on these lessons on at least two occasions after the Showa depression: when fostering the machinery industry as the nucleus of the munitions industry during World War II, and when fostering the export-oriented section of the machinery industry after the war.

The banks were unlikely to be interested in all aspects of the policy of promoting the automotive industry, for example they were not likely to care whether or not the industry was based on specialization. However, it was clear that they were interested in whether the policy would be favourable to their customers, including trading companies.

During the recession of 1951–52, banks facing serious difficulties not only asked MITI and the financial authorities for help but also expressed a desire to work together with MITI. Mitsui Bank, the main bank for Toyota Motors, was a case in point. It did not have sufficient resources to finance car manufacturers but was as keen as MITI to foster the automotive industry. The banks also wanted to rehabilitate trading companies that had been damaged by the recession, and to help them become prominent general trading companies with a close relationship with the heavy and chemical industries. Fuji Bank, the main bank for Nissan Motors was most active in this respect.

In 1961 MITI devised a plan to divide passenger car makers into three groups, with each group specializing in one type of car: mass-produced cars, special-purpose vehicles and mini-cars.[23] In effect MITI wanted only Toyota and Nissan (or three companies including Toyota and Nissan) to manufacture mass-produced cars.

It seems that of the large commercial banks, Fuji Bank was the most positive supporter of MITI's policy. This was because it wished to establish a prominent trading company under its wing that would rank with the Mitsubishi Corporation and Mitsui and Company. Although Mitsui Bank held a smaller volume of deposits than Fuji Bank, it had succeeded in reestablishing Mitsui and Company (first as Daiichi Bussan in 1955 and then as Mitsui and Company in 1959) as one of the most powerful Japanese trading companies. (Despite this the bank was unable to recover the place it had held before the Mitsui zaibatsu had been dissolved, or at least not for the time being. The total deficit of these companies consolidated into Mitsui and Company was huge and Mitsui Bank was shouldering part of this deficit.) By contrast, although Fuji Bank ranked first among the commercial banks in both deposits and the profits arising from foreign exchange business, the Marubeni Corporation (then the Marubeni Iida Corporation), which Fuji Bank had established, was not as powerful as Mitsui and Company and the Mitsubishi Corporation.

In those days it was essential for trading companies to attract the best customers in the steel, machinery, petroleum and petrochemical industries and to develop support activities in these fields if they were to become prominent general trading companies. For Marubeni this was even more essential because it had previously been a cotton trading specialist and had few good customers in heavy industry.

Bearing this in mind, we shall return to MITI's policy of fostering the automotive industry. Because car manufacturers were big consumers of steel and because the general trading companies wanted to increase their businesses with major steel companies it was natural for them to try to extend their influence over car manufacturers as promisingly large consumers of steel. In addition trade in cars could be expected to increase the import and export business of the overseas offices of general trading companies. According to Huang Xio Chun it was necessary for general trading companies to establish a strong network of overseas offices if they were to be superior to manufacturers in the business of foreign trade. As far as Marubeni was concerned, it was able to expand its steel business and strengthen its overseas offices by making Nissan a good customer.[24] For example Marubeni strengthened its Los Angeles office by sharing with Mitsubishi the exclusive right to sell Nissan cars in the US – the former enjoying this right in the western part of the US and the latter in the eastern part until the 1970s.[25]

Summary

During the 1956–57 boom, to win the leading competition Japan's six largest banks focused on cementing their ties with major and promising companies. To survive the even fiercer competition after the 1958 recession they concentrated on meeting their customers' demand for funds, which involved asking other financial institutions to share the burden of providing long-term loans to major companies. The banks' strategies were also followed by the Industrial Bank of Japan.

To secure their status as main bank and/or main creditor the commercial banks set up regular presidents' meetings and cross-shareholdings, which also served as a hedge against the competition that was expected to result from the long-term credit institutions' agreement to share the burden of providing loans to their customers. These precautions were aimed more at preventing other financial institutions from coming to treat such transactions as a continuing vested right than at preventing major customers from being poached by these institutions.

By establishing a network of financial institutions specializing in long-term lending – such as government financial institutions, long-term credit banks and trust banks – the Ministry of Finance was able to promote the smooth provision of funds to major companies.

The Ministry of International Trade and Industry played its part in industrial policy by fostering certain industries – including the Japanese automotive industry – in cooperation with the specialized financial institutions, headed by the Industrial Bank of Japan, and taking the lead in adjusting the supply and demand of long-term capital loans.

6
Dashing into Long-Term Capital Lending, 1966–73

The threat to main bank status

In the late 1960s Mitsui Bank decided to enter long-term capital lending in its own right, to take the first step towards resuming its securities business, which banks had been prohibited from engaging in by a law aimed at putting a wall between the securities and banking sectors, and to continue to deepen the cross-shareholdings between itself and its customers. This was because it wanted to set itself free from the restrictions placed on it as a commercial bank and pursue a lending policy based on well-balanced foundations, and to forge closer links with customers by offering such services.

Mitsui and the other major commercial banks were becoming more and more cautious about asking other financial institutions to share the burden of making loans to their customers, and eventually they decided to discontinue this practice. Their decision seems to have been triggered by a number of high-profile corporate mergers that had had an adverse effect on their activities. The most important mergers were those of Mitsui and Company and Kinoshita and Company in 1965 and Nissan Motors and Prince Motors in 1966. Although Mitsui and Company's main bank was Mitsui Bank and the company was one of the leading members of the Second Thursday Club, it carried out its merger with Kinoshita in cooperation with Fuji Bank without ever consulting Mitsui Bank. Similarly, while Nissan Motors' main bank was Fuji Bank and it was a member of the Fuyo Group, the company merged with Prince Motors in cooperation with the Industrial Bank of Japan rather than Fuji Bank. There is no doubt that these mergers caused strong antagonism between the main bank and Fuji Bank in the former case and the IBJ in the latter case. The main banks had previously asked Fuji Bank and the IBJ to share the burden of providing loans to their customers.

The story behind the merger of Mitsui and Company and Kinoshita is as follows. Mitsui and other general trading companies were well-known for remaining stable in times of adverse business conditions, but smaller trading companies that tended to specialize in certain merchandise lines were so hard hit in the mid 1960s that many could not recover. One such company was Kinoshita, owned and operated by Shigeru Kinoshita. In 1962 Kinoshita's business receipts had not kept pace with its reckless investment expenditure and its overly hasty effort to change itself from a specialist into a general trading company. Its troubles had multiplied just as business conditions worsened and it fell into dire straits. The company had formulated a plan to reconstruct itself, but it had been too late.

Yawata Iron and Steel, Fuji Iron and Steel (which later merged to form today's Nippon Steel Corporation), Fuji Bank and Mitsubishi Bank were among Kinoshita's most important supporters. After failed merger negotiations with Gosho (a specialist trader) these organizations decided that the best solution would be for a leading general trading company to absorb Kinoshita, with its business ties serving as a guarantee for the huge liabilities it carried. The trading company they approached was Mitsui and Company. The president of Yawata Iron and Steel, Yoshihiro Inayama, played the leading role in the negotiations. Having obtained the support of Shigeru Kinoshita, Fuji Iron and Steel and the banks, Inayama approached Mitsui and Company in August 1964 and promised that if the latter would agree to absorb Kinoshita, in the future both Yawata Iron and Steel and Fuji Iron and Steel would do whatever they could to cooperate with Mitsui. Inayama said that although Kinoshita's liabilities amounted to 5–6 billion yen the company's goodwill was worth approximately 3 billion yen, which put the actual liabilities at around 2–3 billion yen. Mitsui's representatives included Yasutaro Niizeki (chairman of the board of directors) and Tatsuzo Mizukami (president). They told Inayama at the close of the first meeting that they were in favour of the merger and an official memorandum was issued to this effect on 27 August 1964, just ten days after Inayama's initial approach to Mitsui.[1]

Thereafter Mitsui's iron and steel trade expanded quickly and became the main supporter of the company's growth in the 1960s. Immediately after the reestablishment of Mitsui and Company in 1959 iron and steel had been competing with foodstuffs for top position, and by March 1965 they had gained that position. Hence the absorption of Kinoshita, which specialized in these products, made Mitsui much more powerful in that field. Mitsui's iron and steel trade underwent tremendous growth both domestically and overseas, with meaningful support activities in the financial, transportation, information and related fields.[2]

As stated above, Mitsui and Company consulted Fuji Bank rather than its main bank, Mitsui Bank, about its merger with Kinoshita. Indeed Mitsui Bank's official history does not even refer to the merger. Interestingly, nor does Mitsui and Company's official history refer to the Second Thursday Club, and the continuation of the company's relationship with Fuji Bank suggests that it had no respect for the part played by the club, which had been established in 1961 under the bank's guidance.

During 1966–75 Mitsui Bank followed two main strategies: at home it attempted to draw closer to the general public, and overseas it promoted the internationalization of its business.[3] Concerning the former, between 1966 and 1970 Japan's economic growth slowly changed from high dependence on private investment in plant and equipment to greater emphasis on slow but stable growth in personal consumption and government expenditure – the growth pattern of an advanced modern economy. The per capita earnings structure changed as the middle class grew to account for 90 per cent of the population, thus forming a new market that banks came to view as an important source of funds and target for loans. Banks offered a wide variety of new services to cater for this segment and were even criticized for 'turning themselves into department stores'.[4]

This strategy seems to have been the successor to the expansion of loans to promising small and medium-sized companies towards the end of the 1950s, when the competition to attract new borrowers took place among the largest banks. In accordance with this strategy Mitsui Bank began to increase its loans, including long-term ones, to individuals as well as to promising small and medium-sized companies. As these loans were accompanied by an increase in deposits, this loan expansion did much towards mitigating the bank's fund shortage problem as well as winning the lending competition from the late 1960s.

With regard to the bank's overseas strategy, since its customers included a large number of corporations that were becoming international or multinational in nature, it had to expand its overseas network in order to meet their growing and diverse needs. The two main areas of business were trade financing and the buying and selling of the foreign currency that accompanied trade.[5] In August 1972 the bank reorganized its overseas department into two divisions: the international division and the international business administration division. Later, in August 1975, it set up an autonomous international finance division and these three divisions became responsible for all the bank's overseas affairs.[6]

Returning to general banking affairs at home, Nissan Motor's merger with Prince Motors in 1966 had such a great impact on Japan's largest commercial banks that they asked the government to abolish its protection of long-term financial institutions, based on the separation of long-term lending from short-term lending. The important point is that until then the IBJ had been to Nissan Motors what Fuji Bank had been to Daiichi Bussan until the beginning of the 1950s. Just as Mitsui and Company's official history misleadingly describes Fuji Bank as Daiichi Bussan's main bank instead of Mitsui Bank, so Nissan Motors' history wrongly refers to the IBJ as Nissan's main bank rather than Fuji Bank,[7] although the IBJ did help Nissan to merge with some other minor automotive companies in the late 1960s. Interestingly the IBJ has also described itself as Nissan's main bank.

The events leading up to the merger were as follows. In light of the expected reorganization of the automotive industry Shojiro Ishibashi (chairman of Prince Motors' board of directors) and Shozo Hotta (president of Sumitomo Bank), as the largest shareholders, and the Ministry of International Trade and Industry became concerned about Prince Motors' future and decided it should merge with another leading automotive company. In March 1965 Yoshio Sakurauchi (minister of international trade and industry) sounded out Katsuji Kawamata (president of Nissan Motors) about a possible merger between Nissan and Prince. During the final stage of the negotiations the IBJ (Nissan's main bank) and Sumitomo Bank (Prince's main bank) decided on the preparation that Prince would receive of the new Nissan Motors' total shares, the selection of officers and so on.[8] Eventually the merger agreement was signed on 31 May 1965 by Kawamata, Ishibashi, the president of Prince, Sohei Nakayama and Hotta (the latter two representing the two companies' main banks respectively). The two companies formally merged on 1 August the following year.[9]

Nissan and Prince's merger was one of the most striking successes of the cooperation between MITI and private companies. Previously, in 1963–64, the competition between car manufacturers to boost their market share by increasing their range of models had intensified in response to the rapid expansion of the domestic market for cars, contrary to MITI's desire to prevent any increase in the number of models available and the entry of new companies into the industry.[10]

The IBJ's share of long-term loans to the heavy and chemical industries in total outstanding long-term loans rose from 47.2 per cent at the end of March 1966 to 50.5 per cent at the end of March 1971, and loans to the automotive industry rose from 4.4 per cent to 6.2 per cent. This was largely the result of the bank's assistance to core companies such as Nissan Motors during the industry's reorganization. The bank also continued to provide substantial loans to the steel industry, as one of Japan's basic industries, and the growing petrochemical industry, and had pluralistic ties with other industries.[11]

The invasion of the commercial banks' territory by the IBJ

The IBJ, which in the 1960s successfully maintained the healthy loan composition it had established in the preceding decade, began to face sharp criticism of its aggressive lending activities by the large commercial banks, which were seeking to expand their own long-term capital lending business. The bank became entangled in a hard-fought lending competition between it and the largest commercial banks, triggered by a reduction in long-term borrowing in 1965–66. The Japanese economy was suffering not only from the recession of 1965 but also from the effect of most companies in the heavy and chemical industries taking a pessimistic view of their future. However this pessimism proved unfounded as in 1966 the economy emerged from recession and a long period of improved business conditions commenced.

Although the IBJ's fund position improved during this period (having suffered a shortage for ten years), it faced cuts in investment in plant and equipment by the major companies that formed the core of its customer base. Consequently it set about diversifying its business and seeking promising new customers. In particular it began to provide its customers with medium and long-term operating funds, something it had not done before but now considered to be a primary activity of long-term credit banks.[12]

The bank's official history refers in a rather roundabout way to the criticism by the commercial banks. It claims that as the problem of fund shortages and excessive borrowing by companies took a gradual turn for the better, the largest commercial banks no longer wanted to ask the long-term credit banks to share the burden of providing loans to their affiliated companies. Hence they asked the Ministry of Finance to approve the introduction of two-year time deposits as a new method of fund raising and diversified their activities into trust business and over-the-counter sales of government bonds. Another contributory factor was that in 1965–66 it was predicted that the economy was at the point of turning from high-speed growth to structural recession and future investment in plant and equipment was in question, and therefore help from the long-term credit banks was no longer considered necessary by some of the commercial banks.[13]

Thus in 1967 the large commercial banks decided to reduce their subscription to the IBJ's debentures and to appeal to the government to remove the rigid demarcation lines it had drawn between commercial banks, long-term credit banks and trust banks.[14] Before long they even demanded the abolition of the solid wall between the securities and banking sectors that had been erected by the Securities and Exchange Law.

As Table 6.1 shows, the IBJ's share of total outstanding long-term capital loans fell from 15.6 per cent at the end of March 1966 to 12.4 per cent at the end of March 1974. The lending shares of the long-term credit banks, the Development Bank of Japan and the trust banks (the trust accounts held by trust banks and Daiwa Bank to be exact) also declined, and only the large commercial banks increased their share during this period – from 15.2 per cent to 30.2 per cent. Reflecting this, concerning the large commercial banks, the share of long-term capital loans in total loans (short-term loans

Table 6.1 Main financial institutions' outstanding long-term capital loans, end of March 1966 to end of March 1974 (per cent)

	Long-term credit banks incl. IBJ		IBJ		Large commercial banks		Trust banks		Development Bank of Japan	
	1966	1974	1966	1974	1966	1974	1966	1974	1966	1974
Manufacturing	42.4	37.1	19.2	17.8	11.6	20.4	40.0	36.3	5.8	6.2
Chemicals	41.5	38.0	20.9	22.0	14.4	18.6	33.8	36.2	10.3	7.3
Oil refining	25.8	28.1	11.9	13.1	42.3	28.9	30.2	28.8	1.7	14.2
Steel	43.0	39.7	23.4	18.4	9.5	15.8	44.1	41.1	2.6	3.4
Non-ferrous metals	48.1	44.8	20.0	24.1	5.2	11.2	41.9	34.5	4.7	9.5
Machinery	43.0	36.7	19.9	19.5	5.0	18.4	46.2	39.4	5.9	5.5
(Electrical)	(47.1)	(39.9)	(21.8)	(18.6)	(2.4)	(16.8)	(47.9)	(38.8)	(2.6)	(4.6)
(Cars)	(38.4)	(36.7)	(10.0)	(22.9)	(6.2)	(15.9)	(49.3)	(42.1)	(6.0)	(5.4)
(Shipbuilding)	(45.6)	(39.3)	(22.6)	(19.1)	(1.8)	(12.4)	(47.9)	(40.8)	(4.7)	(7.5)
Textiles	46.7	35.1	17.0	14.3	7.6	18.1	40.1	39.7	5.6	7.1
Non-manufacturing	29.5	23.3	11.9	8.6	18.9	37.1	22.1	24.6	29.5	15.0
Wholesale and retail	44.7	26.2	4.5	6.6	34.4	55.1	20.2	16.2	0.7	2.6
Land transport	30.6	26.0	15.6	12.9	15.4	13.9	47.9	44.9	6.2	15.1
Shipping	14.6	17.7	7.4	7.8	9.8	12.9	4.8	9.7	70.8	59.7
Electric power	28.1	32.1	16.8	19.9	6.1	11.1	21.1	28.6	44.7	28.2
Real estate	38.7	26.8	9.2	6.5	35.8	33.8	23.8	31.6	1.7	7.8
Services	26.6	27.8	3.7	6.3	41.6	49.9	17.4	11.9	14.4	10.4
Share of Total	36.1	29.1	15.6	12.4	15.2	30.2	31.3	29.5	17.4	11.3

Source: Industrial Bank of Japan, The 75 Year History of the Industrial Bank of Japan (Tokyo: Industrial Bank of Japan, 1982), pp. 726, 946.

plus long-term loans) rose from 7.6 per cent at the end of March 1966 to 12.0 per cent at the end of March 1971.

We shall illustrate this point with an example from Fuji Bank. Fuji brought together the largest commercial banks in December 1967 to appeal to the government to scrap the rigid demarcation lines between commercial banks, long-term credit banks and trust banks.[15] It had asked the IBJ to share the burden of providing long-term loans to customers such as Nissan and Hitachi. Its restraint on the provision of long-term loans had given it good access to promising small and medium-sized companies. However it decided to set about expanding this service itself. It will be remembered that Nissan and Hitachi were original members of the Fuyo Group, established in January 1966, and therefore Fuji was clearly these two companies' main bank.

Fuji Bank's overall loans to its customers increased rapidly from 1966 onwards. The concurrent expansion of long-term loans reflected unanticipated private sector investment in plant and equipment. The share of long-term loans in the bank's total outstanding loans rose from about 7.5 per cent at the end of March 1967 to about 14.0 per cent at the end of March 1971.[16] Although the bank reduced its subscriptions to financial bonds and sold some of its bond holdings, its outside debt expanded, exceeding 450 billion yen by the end of March 1971.

From the beginning of the 1970s all the major commercial banks concentrated on expanding their long-term capital lending business, which had suddenly become indispensable to them as failure to provide this service would eventually make it difficult for them to keep their status as main bank for their major customers.

However their focus had to change slightly towards the expansion of medium- and long-term capital banking at home and overseas rather than just concentrating on the expansion of long-term capital lending at home, which they had wanted to be able to do since the 1950s. Their medium- and long-term capital lending in foreign currency swelled and joined their main stream foreign exchange business. In contrast, conducting the foreign exchange business that accompanied trade became extremely difficult as they had to adhere to the rigid demarcation lines drawn by the government between commercial banks, long-term credit banks and trust banks and to a wall between the securities and banking sectors.

In July 1970 the Financial System Research Council's Special Committee on Private Financial Institutions, an advisory organ, submitted to the minister of finance a document entitled 'How Private Financial Institutions Should Be' after heated discussions that had lasted about two and a half years. In line with the committee's recommendations, commercial banks were given approval to expand their long-term capital lending business on condition that they did not jeopardize the functioning of the long-term credit institutions, and *vice versa*.[17]

This conditional approval meant that the large commercial banks and the long-term credit institutions, headed by the IBJ, had at last managed to work out a compromise under the guidance of the Ministry of Finance, which was attempting to make the financial sector more efficient in preparation for the liberalization of capital inflows and outflows. The financial sector as a whole had to think in the same way as the ministry about how to reorganize the sector so that it could cope efficiently with the attempt by industries to strengthen their international competitiveness.[18]

As noted above, when the large commercial banks turned their attention to international financing and long-term capital lending to promising small and medium-sized companies and individuals they had to take into account not only their customers' demand for funds but also the conflict of interests between them and the long-term credit institutions. Furthermore the monetary conditions at the time (which were similar to those which later prevailed during the bubble economy of the late 1980s) were such that the large commercial banks soon became aware that these businesses were both risky and profitable. These conditions emerged in August 1971 when US President Nixon announced emergency economic measures such as the end of dollar–gold convertibility and a demand that Japan and other countries running large international current account surpluses revalue their currencies.

According to Takafusa Nakamura, Japan managed to preserve a fixed exchange rate of 360 yen to the dollar for almost two weeks, but on 28 August it had to change to a floating system. Foreign exchange banks and large trading companies took advantage of the interval between Nixon's announcement and 28 August to turn all their dollars into yen at the fixed rate. This caused heavy losses for the Bank of Japan, which recorded an unprecedented deficit.[19] On the other hand, according to Mitsui Bank's official history, as one of Japan's leading foreign exchange banks Mitsui won high regard for its wise handling of the large volume of dollars it was requested to buy from Japanese trading companies during the monetary confusion that reigned that month.[20]

In December 1971 the Smithsonian Agreement, signed by the finance ministers of twelve major nations, set the exchange rate for the yen at 308 to the dollar, a 16.88 per cent revaluation. (Later, in March 1973, the Smithsonian Agreement collapsed and Japan returned to a floating rate of 257–264 yen to the dollar, which constituted a revaluation of 17–20 per cent.) Anticipating the damage that the yen's revaluation would inflict on the economy the government, in consultation with the Bank of Japan, decided to increase fiscal spending and public works investment and to relax its monetary policy, resulting in excess liquidity.[21]

Under such monetary conditions the large commercial banks' fund positions improved, as did those of the IBJ and other financial institutions. In 1972 an aggressive competition to provide long-term capital loans to companies broke out among these banks. (As noted above, the large commercial banks' share of the total outstanding long-term capital loans of the major financial institutions rose dramatically from 21.0 per cent on 31 March 1971 to 30.2 per cent on 31 March 1974, while that of the long-term credit banks dipped slightly.) The commercial banks' loan expansion mainly involved non-manufacturing companies, particularly in the wholesale and retail, construction and service sectors, whose share of such loans rose from 60.5 per cent to 71.7 per cent. Most of these borrowers were small and medium-sized companies.

Summary

In the late 1960s Japan's large commercial banks decided to cease asking other financial institutions to share the burden of providing loans to their customers and to set about expanding their long-term capital lending business. However this was not taken very far as the economy began to enjoy a long period of improved business conditions.

It was certain that they decided to do so because their fund shortage problems were relieved and they were able to fulfill themselves as main banks. But it is important to know that there were other factors urging them to make such a decision.

One was the completion of several high-profile corporate mergers (such as that between Mitsui and Company and Kinoshita) that threatened to jeopardize the main bank status of the banks concerned. The other was the specialized financial institutions' rush to diversify their business. In particular the IBJ was eager to venture into the commercial banks' territory, based on a new lending strategy to attract promising customers. The bank liberally provided its customers with medium and long-term operating funds, which it had not been able to do before.

From the beginning of the 1970s the large commercial banks dashed into long-term lending. They were forced to put special emphasis on international financing and long-term capital lending to promising small and medium-sized companies and individuals, taking into account not only their customers' demand for funds but also the conflict of interest between themselves and the long-term credit institutions.

7
Conclusion

In the prewar years Mitsui Bank, in its effort to become a genuine commercial bank, gave preference to the discounting of commercial bills over loans on bills, and to short-term lending over long-term capital lending. When putting this into practice it attached great importance to conducting foreign exchange business with such major trading companies as Mitsui and Company and to securities operations on behalf of major debtors.

Prior to the outbreak of war between Japan and China in 1937 the bank mainly succeeded in keeping the average loan period to within two months, but had to meet the demand for longer-term capital funds by Mitsui-affiliated companies, electric power companies and others. The average loan period increased when it expanded its loans to electric power companies in the periods 1926–27 and 1930–33. It was able to do so mainly by underwriting bonds issued by the power companies to pay off their loans.

This combining of securities business with lending business was extended to the financing of munitions companies, and in this way the bank was able to keep the loan period to within two months even after 1937. However it became increasingly difficult for it to do this because of the shrinkage of its foreign exchange and securities business. By the beginning of the 1940s Teikoku Bank, established through the merger of Dai-Ichi Bank and Mitsui Bank, was facing a serious fund shortage problem and virtually had to abandon the provision of long-term loans, despite the government's call for commercial banks to increase such provision.

Thanks to the dissolution of the zaibatsu immediately after World War II, Teikoku Bank (in 1948 redivided into Mitsui Bank and Dai-Ichi Bank) and other zaibatsu-affiliated banks were set free from the control of the zaibatsu families. As a result they became able to act as lender of last resort for major companies, including former zaibatsu affiliates, at their own discretion.

In the postwar years Japan's six largest commercial banks, comprising mainly the former zaibatsu-affiliated banks, abandoned their policy of keeping customers at arm's length and began to group the largest and most promising of their customers around them as main banks. Six corporate groupings headed by these banks came into existence in the early 1950s. In order to carry out this policy successfully it was essential for them to offer long-term capital loans. However they failed to do so and instead engaged in the provision of short-term loans and the discounting of commercial bills and especially foreign bills of exchange for major trading companies. In particular they tried to increase the proportion of loans to wholesalers in order to construct a balanced loan composition by industry.

While concentrating on short-term loans they asked other financial institutions to share the burden of providing large-scale, long-term capital funds to their customers in the heavy and chemical industries. This provided an added incentive to strengthen the corporate groupings, both as a means to put loan prioritization into practice and as a guard against other financial institutions encroaching on their relationship with the companies in question.

The share of long-term capital loans in total outstanding loans at Mitsui Bank was higher than that of any other of Japan's six largest banks at the end of March 1956, peaking at 12.7 per cent at the end of 1958. Such a rise in the share during the years 1956–58 got its average loan period fairly long, though the share of long-term capital loans in total outstanding loans at Mitsui at the end of 1958 was considerably below what it had been at the end of 1937 (20.6 per cent – The bank's average loan period had been 1.63 months in the second half of 1937 and 1.72 months in the first half of 1938). Between the end of September 1955 and the end of March 1957 the share of outstanding loans with a term of two months or less decreased and the share of loans with a term of over 12 months increased considerably. However the average loan period for the other large banks had changed only slightly during the same period, with 80 per cent of loans having a term of three months or less.

During the early 1960s Mitsui Bank continued to base its operations on the establishment of a well-balanced business foundation and the formation of firm ties with companies, rather than engaging in long-term capital lending and securities. The bank established the Second Thursday Club – regular scheduled meetings between the presidents of client companies – and cross-shareholdings between the bank and its major customers in the hope that this would boost transactions between important trading companies (Mitsui and Company in particular) and its principal customers in the heavy and chemical industries and that such transactions would help the bank to maintain its high percentage share of loans to wholesalers (mainly general trading companies). The meetings and cross-shareholdings were also a useful means of protecting its status as the main bank of its customers. This was also true of rival commercial banks, which had introduced similiar arrangements.

Mitsui and the other commercial banks became more cautious about asking other financial institutions to share the burden of providing loans to their customers when the lending competition among these banks and between them and the IBJ became intense. (In 1952 the IBJ had been turned into a private bank specializing in long-term capital lending, and like the commercial banks it had set about grouping together its largest and most promising customers, with itself at the centre as their main bank.) However the IBJ continued to act as a complement to the commercial banks by providing long-term capital loans, as before.

Although IBJ did not set up regular meetings with the presidents of its major customers it took other measures analogous to such meetings in order to strengthen its links with these customers and win the lending competition. The bank's other activities were mainly aimed at reorganizing the major industries, cutting down their capital expenditure programmes and reducing their demand for long-term loans. This was done in cooperation with the government departments in charge of financial and industrial policies.

During the late 1960s Mitsui and the other major commercial banks decided to engage fully in long-term capital lending and to move towards the resumption of their securities business as the provision of these services would enable them to forge closer links with their customers.

From the mid 1970s the large commercial banks and financial institutions such as long-term credit banks and trust banks began to diversify their business, although the target of all of them was to increase their share of long-term capital lending. There is no doubt that such lending competitions damaged the Japanese financial system and the economy as a whole as they led to the excess provision of long-term loans, particularly to real estate developers, and caused relatively weak players to overexpand their international financing business. This resulted in excess capacity among domestic industries and the bubble economy of the late 1980s, and unlike in the favourable years between the late 1970s and the early 1980s monetary problems could not be managed by exporting and investing abroad.

Notes and References

Preface

1. The following are the main studies to re-evaluate the role and function of Japan's commercial banks in their corporate groupings: Juro Hashimoto and Haruhito Takeda (eds), *Nihon Keizai no Hatten to Kigyo Shudan* (Corporate Groupings in the Developing Japanese Economy) (Tokyo: University of Tokyo Press, 1992); Masahiko Aoki and Hugh Patrick (eds), *The Japanese Main Bank System: Its Relevance for Developing and Transforming Economies* (New York: Oxford University Press, 1994); Haruhito Takeda (ed.), *Nihon Sangyo Hatten no Dainamizumu* (The Dynamism of Developing Japanese Industry) (Tokyo: University of Tokyo Press, 1995); Ken Suzuki, *Mein Banku to Kigyo Shudan* (Main Banks and Corporate Groupings) (Kyoto: Minerva Shobo, 1998).

2. For the definition 'main bank' I shall follow Satoshi Sunamura, a senior managing director at Barclays Bank plc in Tokyo: 'Prima facie, the honour of main bank status is normally given to the largest lending bank which not only keeps a relatively high share of equity holding on its own account, but also influences corporate governance because of the de facto equity cross-holding among group companies and often through the bank's representation on the corporate board. But, it is not always the case that the largest lender is the main bank.... In fact, the real qualification for main bank status depends on the bank's ability to undertake restructuring or to bear the ultimate credit risk of clients. Such an undertaking is only possible if it is based upon extensive credit appraisal as well as careful monitoring of corporate performance. For this reason, the major qualifications of a main bank must be endorsed by practical managerial capacity in the ex ante, interim, and ex post relationships with clients. The real qualification of the main bank is whether it is ready to act as the lender of last resort when a borrower faces difficulty, even though it has not been formally contracted to do so.' Satoshi Sunamura, 'The Development of Main Bank Managerial Capacity', in Aoki and Patrick' *The Japanese Main Bank System*, op. cit., pp. 296–8.

Introduction

1. Alfred D. Chandler Jr, *Scale and Scope: the dynamics of industrial capitalism* (Cambridge, Mass.: Harvard University Press, 1990), p. 389.
2. Ibid., pp. 418–19.
3. Ibid., p. 389.
4. Ibid., p. 81.
5. Hidemasa Morikawa, *Zaibatsu: the rise and fall of family enterprise groups in Japan* (Tokyo: University of Tokyo Press, 1992), p. 93.

6. Ibid., p. 182.
7. Ibid., pp. 96–8.

1   Mitsui Bank under the Control of the Mitsui Family

1. These descriptions are based on the following: Mitsui Bank, *The Mitsui Bank: A History of the First 100 Years* (English edition) (Tokyo: Mitsui Bank, 1976), pp. 33–56; Fuji Bank, *Fuji Bank 1880–1980* (English edition) (Tokyo: Fuji Bank, 1980), p. 9.
2. Mitsui Bank, op. cit., p. 60.
3. Ibid., pp. 64–5.
4. Ibid., p. 68.
5. Hidemasa Morikawa, *Zaibatsu: the rise fall of family enterprise groups in Japan* (Tokyo: University of Tokyo Press, 1992), p. 65.
6. Ibid., p. 100.
7. Ibid., p. 101. Among the graduates of the Tokyo Higher Commercial College and its predecessors, Senjiro Watanabe assumed the top position at Mitsui and Company when Masuda left in 1904 to become full-time executive director of the control department of the Mitsui Family Council.
8. Mitsui Bank, *The Mitsui Bank*, op. cit., p. 68.
9. Mitsui Bunko (Mitsui Research Institute for Social and Economic History, hereafter MRISEH) (ed.), *Mitsui Jigyo Shi* (The History of Mitsui Business Enterprises), vol. 3, pt 1 (Tokyo: MRISEH, 1980), pp. 3–22.
10. Mitsui Bank, *The Mitsui Bank*, op. cit., p. 68.
11. Mitsui Bank, 'Minutes of the Branch Managers' Meeting held in October 1904', in Nihon Keieishi Kenkyusho (Japan Business History Institute, hereafter JBHI) (ed.), *Mitsui Ginko Shiryo* (Historical Materials on Mitsui Bank), vol. 2 (Tokyo: JBHI, 1977), p. 84; Mitsui Family Council, 'Minutes of the Council's Control Department', pt 1, in MRISEH (ed.), *Mitsui Bunko Ronso* (*Mitsui Research Institute Review*), no. 7 (Tokyo: MRISEH, 1973), p. 335.
12. Mitsui Bank, *The Mitsui Bank*, op. cit., pp. 69–70.
13. Ibid., p. 63.
14. 'Memoirs of Tomozo Toyama' in 'Memoirs of ex-Executives of Mitsui Bank (unpublished collection in the Sakura Bank archives).
15. Mitsui Bank, 'Minutes of the Branch Managers' Meeting held in November 1908', in JBHI (ed.), *Historical Materials on Mitsui Bank*, vol. 3 (Tokyo: JBHI, 1977), pp. 60–3, 265–6.
16. 'Memoirs of Tomozo Toyama', op. cit.
17. *Yoneyama Umekichi Den* (The Life of Umekichi Yoneyama) (Tokyo: Aoyama Gakuin Shotobu, 1960), p. 311.
18. Kiichiro Sato, *Ori ni Furete* (My Reminiscences), pt 2 (Tokyo: Institute for Banking and Financial Research, 1962), p. 118.
19. 'Memoirs of Shigeo Katayama', in 'Memoirs of ex-Executives of Mitsui Bank', op. cit.

20. MRISEH, *The History of Mitsui Business Enterprises*, vol. 2 (Tokyo: MRISEH, 1980), p. 576; Kiyohide Narita, *Oji Seishi Shashi* (The History of Oji Paper Co.) (Tokyo: Oji Paper, 1958), pp. 47–9.
21. Mitsui Bank, 'Minutes of the Branch Managers' Meeting held in October 1913', in JBHI (ed.), *Historical Materials on Mitsui Bank*, vol. 4 (Tokyo: JBHI, 1977), p. 7.
22. The Mitsui Family Council, 'Minutes of the Council's Control Department', in MRISEH (ed.), *Mitsui Research Institute Review*, vol. 9 (Tokyo: MRISEH, 1975), pp. 377, 379. On the disposal of Shibaura Electric Works in the 1900s, see Toshiba, *Shibaura Seisakusho 65-nen Shi* (The 65 Year History of Shibaura Electric Works) (Tokyo: Toshiba, 1940), chs 3 and 4; 'Minutes of Mitsui-Related Companies' Executives' Meetings', in MRISEH (ed.), *Mitsui Jigyoshi Shiryohen* (Historical Materials on the History of Mitsui Business Enterprises), vol. 4, pt 2 (Tokyo: MRISEH, 1972), pp. 697–711; Hidemasa Morikawa, *Zaibatsu no Keieishiteki Kenkyu* (Studies in the Business History of the Zaibatsu) (Tokyo: Toyo Keizai Shimposha, 1980), pp. 43–58.
23. Industrial Bank of Japan, *Nihon Kogyo Ginko 50-nen Shi* (The 50 Year History of the Industrial Bank of Japan) (Tokyo: Industrial Bank of Japan, 1957), pp. 123–34.
24. Mitsui Bank, 'Minutes of the Branch Managers' Meeting held in November 1908', op. cit., p. 260.
25. Mitsui Bank, 'Minutes of the Branch Managers' Meeting held in October 1913', op. cit., p. 204.
26. Mitsui and Company, Semi-Annual Reports for 1917 (unpublished documents in the MRISEH archives); Shinji Ogura, *Senzenki Mitsui Ginko Kigyotorihiki Kankeishi no Kenkyu* (Mitsui Bank and Its Customers 1900–43) (Tokyo: Sembundo, 1990), pp. 128–34.
27. Mitsui Bank, *The Mitsui Bank*, op. cit., pp. 81–2.
28. 'Memoirs of Tomozo Toyama', op. cit.
29. Sumitomo Bank, *Sumitomo Ginko 80-nen Shi* (The 80 Year History of Sumitomo Bank) (Osaka: Sumitomo Bank, 1979), pp. 195–201.
30. 'Memoirs of Tomozo Toyama', op. cit.
31. 'Memoirs of Hirokichi Kameshima', in 'Memoirs of ex-Executives of Mitsui Bank', op. cit.
32. Mitsui Bank, 'Directives from the head office' (unpublished documents in the Sakura Bank archives).
33. Mitsui Bank, *The Mitsui Bank: A Brief History, Jubilee Commemoration 1926* (English edition) (Tokyo: Mitsui Bank, 1927), pp. 65–72.
34. Mitsui Bank, *The Mitsui Bank: A History of the First 100 Years'* op. cit., p. 96.
35. Mitsui Bank, 'Telegrams on the Bank's Fund Position', in JBHI (ed.), *Historical Materials on Mitsui Bank*, vol. 5 (Tokyo: JBHI, 1978); Mitsui Bank, Minutes of the Board of Directors', no. 859 (14 May 1920), no. 860 (28 May 1920), no. 864 (23 July 1920) (unpublished); Mitsui and Company, 'Minutes of the 8th Branch Managers' Meeting,' MRISEH archives; Mitsui Mining, Semi-Annual Reports.

36. Mitsui Bank, 'directives from the head office', op. cit.
37. Mitsui Bank, *The Mitsui Bank: A History of the First 100 Years'* op. cit., p. 95; *The Secret Story of and Documents on Mitsui Bank*, 4 vols (Sakura Bank archives, unpublished); Mitsui Bank, 'Minutes of the Board of Directors', no. 859, op. cit., Mitsui Bank, supplement to the *Hochi* (the bank's internal newspaper), no. 2421 (27 April 1920).
38. Mitsui Bank, 'Minutes of the General Managers' Meeting', especially the minutes of the meeting' on 25 February 1930 (Sakura Bank archives).
39. Mitsui Bank, *The Mitsui Bank: A History of the First 100 Years*, op. cit., p. 88.
40. *The Secret Story of and Documents on Mitsui Bank*, op. cit.
41. Mitsui Bank, 'Telegrams on the Bank's Fund Position', op. cit.; Mitsui Bank, semi-annual reports to the Mitsui Gomei (a holding company), especially the reports for 1923–26 (Sakura Bank archives).
42. Mitsui Bank, *The Mitsui Bank: A History of the First 100 Years*, op. cit., p. 89.
43. Seiji Moroo, *Jigyo Kinyu Jimbutsu: Daido Denryoku 20-nen Kinyushi Kou* (Business, Finance and Leading Figures: A Study of Daido Electric Power Co.'s Capital Raising for 20 Years) (Nishinomiya, Hyogo Prefecture: Seiji Moroo, 1940), pp. 89–241 especially pp. 271–3.
44. Mitsui Bank, New York Branch, 'Report on an Investigation into Investment Bankers', 1925, (unpublished document in the Sakura Bank archives). According to this report the bank first negotiated with the Bankers Trust Company for the latter to underwrite bonds. These negotiations, however, ended in failure.
45. US Senate Committee on Finance, *Sale of Foreign Bonds or Securities in the United States* (Washington, DC: Government Printing Office, 1931–32), p. 959.
46. Mitsui Bank, 'directives from the head office', op. cit.
47. Mitsui Bank, *Mitsui Ginko 80-nen Shi* (The 80 Year History of Mitsui Bank) (Tokyo: Mitsui Bank, 1957), p. 419.
48. *The Secret Story of and Documents on Mitsui Bank*, op. cit.
49. Mitsui Bank, *The Mitsui Bank: A History of the First 100 Years*, op. cit., p. 93.
50. Mitsui Bank, semi-annual reports to the Mitsui Gomei, especially the reports for 1927–29 (Sakura Bank archives).
51. Ibid. especially the report for the second half of 1927 (Sakura Bank archives); 'Mitsui Bank,' Minutes of the Board of Directors', no. 1036 (8 July 1927).
52. Mitsui Bank, 'Documents on the Bank's Large Substantial Credit to Customers', (Sakura Bank archives, unpublished); *The Secret Story of and Documents on Mitsui Bank*, op. cit.
53. US Senate Committee on Finance, *Sale of Foreign Bonds*, op. cit., pp. 959–62, 1082–1111.
54. Mitsui Bank, 'Telegrams on the Bank's Fund Position', op. cit., pp. 274–317; Mitsui Bank, semi-annual reports to the Mitsui Gomei, especially the reports for 1927–29 (Sakura Bank archives).

2 Towards a Closer Relationship with Industry

1. Fuji Bank, *Fuji Bank 1880–1980* (English edition) (Tokyo: Fuji Bank, 1980), p. 17; Takafusa Nakamura, *A History of Showa Japan, 1926–1989* (Tokyo: University of Tokyo Press, 1998), pp. 46–7, 71, 106, 149, 232–5. (this book was originally published in Japanese in 1993 in two volumes); Mitsui Bank, *The Mitsui Bank: A History of First 100 Years* (Tokyo: Mitsui Bank, 1976), pp. 106–7.
2. Tametsugu Hagiwara, *Suppadaka ni shita Koshu Zaibatsu* (The Naked Truth About the Koshu Zaibatsu) (Tokyo: Tametsugu Hagiwara, 1932), pp. 502–7; Tokyo Electric Light Company, *Tokyo Dento Kabushiki Kaisha Kaigyo 50-nen Shi* (The 50 Year History of the Tokyo Electric Light Company) (Tokyo: Tokyo Electric Light Co., 1936), pp. 165–82; *The Secret Story of and Documents on Mitsui Bank*, 4 vols (Sakura Bank archives, unpublished).
3. 'Memoirs of Naojiro Kikumoto', in 'Memoirs of ex-Executives of Mitsui Bank' (Sakura Bank archives).
4. Seihin Ikeda, *Zaikai Kaiko* (Memoirs of the Japanese Business Circle) (Tokyo: Sekai no Nihonsha, 1949), pp. 230–1.
5. *Tokyo Asahi Shimbun* (Tokyo newspaper), news reports from April and May 1930.
6. *Inoue Junnosuke Den* (The Life of Junnosuke Inoue) (Tokyo: Inoue Junnosuke Ronso Hensankai, 1935), pp. 607–10.
7. *Asahi Keizai Nenshi* (The Asahi Economic Chronicle) (Osaka: Asahi Shimbunsha, 1932), pp. 112–25.
8. Mitsui Bank, 'Minutes of the Branch Managers' Meeting held in October 1929', in JBHI (ed.), *The History of Mitsui Business Enterprises*, vol. 4 (Tokyo: JBHI, 1977), p. 702.
9. Mitsui and Company, 'Minutes of the 10th Branch Managers' Meeting', 1931 (MRISEH archives, unpublihsed), pp. 158–9.
10. Ministry of International Trade and Industry (ed.), *Shoko Seisaku Shi* (The History of the Ministry's Industrial and Commercial Policies), vol. 9 (Tokyo: Ministry of International Trade and Industry, 1961), pp. 12–31.
11. Mitsui Bank, 'Minutes of the General Managers' Meetings', (Sakura Bank archives).
12. Mitsui Bank, semi-annual reports to the Mitsui Gomei, especially the report for the first half of 1931 (Sakura Bank archives).
13. Ibid., especially the report for the second half of 1931.
14. *The Secret Story of and Documents on Mitsui Bank*, op. cit.
15. Ikeda, *Zaikai Kaiko* op. cit., p. 162.
16. Nakamura, *A History of Showa Japan*, op. cit., pp. 84, 87.
17. Mitsui Bank, semi-annual reports to the Mitsui Gomei, especially the report for the second half of 1931 (Sakura Bank archives).
18. Tokyo Electric Light Company, *The 50 year History*, op. cit., pp. 202–9.
19. *The Secret Story of and Documents on Mitsui Bank*, op. cit.
20. Mitsui Bank, 'An Investigation into the Bank's Loans to Mitsui-Related Companies and These Executives', in JBHI (ed.), *Historical Materials on Mitsui Bank*, vol. 5 (Tokyo: JBHI, 1978), pp. 543–4.

21. Mitsui Bank, semi-annual reports to the Mitsui Gomei, especially the reports from the first half of 1932 to the first half of 1934 (Sakura Bank archives).
22. Mitsui Bank, 'A Summary of the Chairman's Address to the Branch Managers' Meeting held on 2 October 1935', in Mitsui Bank, 'The Collected Chairman's Addresses to the Branch Managers' Meetings' (Sakura Bank archives, unpublished).
23. Mitsui Bank, *The 80 Year History of Mitsui Bank* (Tokyo: Mitsui Bank, 1957), especially, its chronicle.
24. Mitsui Bank, 'An Investigation', op. cit., pp. 538–9, 547–8.
25. Mitsui Bank, *The Mitsui Bank: A History of the First 100 Years* (Tokyo: Mitsui Bank, 1976), p. 105.
26. Ibid., p. 102.
27. Mitsui Bank, 'Monthly Reports of the Bank's Transactions with Mitsui-Related Companies in Loans and Deposits', in JBHI (ed.), *Historical Materials on Mitsui Bank*, op. cit., pp. 564–87; Mitsui Bank, 'Documents on the Bank's Substantial Credit to Customers' (Sakura Bank archives, unpublished); Mitsui Bank, 'The Bank's Audit Report for the First Quarter of 1943' (Sakura Bank archives, unpublished).
28. Kuni Sasaki (ed.), *Arishihi Hitotoshite no Mandai Junshiro* (The Life of Junshiro Mandai and His Personality) (Yokosuka: Toshi Mandai, 1964), pp. 401–2, 426, 431.
29. 'Memoirs of Junshiro Mandai', in 'Memoirs of ex-Executives of Mitsui Bank', (Sakura Bank archives).
30. Ibid.; Mitsui Bank, 'An Investigation into the Bank's Loans Provided as Capital Funds', in JBHI (ed.), *Historical Materials on Mitsui Bank*, op. cit., pp. 551, 559, 563; Mitsui Bank, 'Minutes of the Board of Directors', no. 1295 (10 September 1937).
31. Sasaki, *Arishihi Hitotoshite no Mandai Junshiro*, op. cit., pp. 430, 433; Mitsui Bank, *The 80 Year History*, op. cit., p. 272; 'Memoirs of Junshiro Mandai', op. cit.
32. 'Memoirs of Junshiro Mandai', op. cit.; Mitsui Bank, *The 80 Year History*, op. cit., p. 281; Dai-Ichi Bank, *Dai-Ichi Ginkoshi Gekan* (The History of Dai-Ichi Bank, vol. 2 (Tokyo: Dai-Ichi Bank, 1958), pp. 318–9.
33. Mitsui Bank, *The Mitsui Bank*, op. cit., p. 107.

3   Teikoku Bank's New Strategy

1. Mitsui Bank, *The 80 Year History of Mitsui Bank* (Tokyo: Mitsui Bank, 1957), pp. 295, 297; Mitsui Bank, 'Collected Chairman's Addresses to the Branch Managers' Meetings' (Sakura Bank archives).
2. Industrial Bank of Japan, *Nihon Kogyo Ginko 50-nen Shi* (The 50 Year History of the Industrial Bank of Japan) (Tokyo: Industrial Bank of Japan, 1957), pp. 575–6.
3. Sumitomo Bank, *The 80 Year History of Sumitomo Bank* (Osaka: Sumitomo Bank, 1979), pp. 334–5.
4. Fuji Bank, *Fuji Ginko 80-nen Shi* (The 80 Year History of Fuji Bank) (Tokyo: Fuji Bank, 1960), p. 196; Fuji Bank, *Fuji Ginko 100-nen Shi* (The 100 Year

History of Fuji Bank) (Tokyo: Fuji Bank, 1982), p. 504. These large commercial banks' move to increase their long-term loans corresponded to
that by banks in the United States after the Great Depression. Tian-Kang
Go, (1999) refers to the emergence of 'term loans' (loans with a maturity
of one to ten years) in the United States. According to Go, until the 1920s
commercial banks generally limited their lending to short-term loans, that
is, loans maturing within six months. However, after the stock market
crash of 1929 some of the large commercial banks began to provide
borrowers with 1–3 year loans. By the end of 1937 the amount of term
loans held by banks reached an estimated $828 000 000, and for some
large banks term lending came to comprise 10 per cent of all loans. As a
method of financing, term loans enjoyed a number of advantages over the
public offering of securities. First, term lending eliminated or reduced the
expenses inevitably incurred when making a public offering. Second, term
loans could be arranged much more quickly than public offerings. Third,
the terms of term loans could be easily modified to meet the changing circumstances of the borrower. Finally, term lending relieved the issuer of the
need for public disclosure, and protected corporate directors from potential civil liabilities under the Securities Act. See Tian-Kang Go, *American
Commercial Banks in Corporate Finance 1929– 1941: A Study in Banking
Concentration* (New York and London: Garland Publishing, 1999), pp. 3–8.

5. Fuji Bank, *The 100 Year History*, op. cit., pp. 503–7.
6. 'Collected Directives from Teikoku Bank's Head Office', pt 1 (Sakura
   Bank archives, unpublished).
7. Ibid.
8. Mitsui Bank, 'Collected Chairman's Addresses', op. cit.
9. 'Documents on Teikoku Bank's operations' (Sakura Bank archives).
10. Mitsubishi Bank, *Mitsubishi Ginkoshi* (The History of Mitsubishi Bank)
    (Tokyo: Mitsubishi Bank, 1954), p. 355.
11. Zenkoku Kinyu Toseikai (The National Finance Control Agency), 'Essential
    Points about the Designated Banks' War Loan Syndication in Progress', in
    Research Division of the Bank of Japan (ed.), *Nihon Kinyushi Shiryo Showa
    Hen* (Materials on Japan's Financial History, the Showa Period), vol. 34
    (Tokyo: Ministry of Finance, 1974), pp. 409–12.
12. 'Collected Directives from Teikoku Bank's Head Office', pt 2 (Sakura
    Bank archives, unpublished).
13. Industrial Bank of Japan, *Nihon Kogyo Ginko 50-nen Shi*, op. cit.,
    pp. 592–3, 597.
14. Teikoku Bank, 'Report of the Department of Examination of Loan
    Applications', in 'Collected Directives from Teikoku Bank's Head Office',
    pt 1 (Sakura Bank archives).

4 Formation of the Mitsui Group through Loan Relationships

1. Fuji Bank, *Fuji Bank* 1880–1980 (Tokyo: Fuji Bank, 1980), pp. 20–1.
2. Fuji Bank, *The 100 Year History of Fuji Bank* (Tokyo: Fuji Bank, 1982),
   pp. 904–5.

3. Ibid., pp. 25–6.
4. Mitsui Bank, *The Mitsui Bank: A History of the First 100 Years* (Tokyo: Mitsui Bank, 1976), pp. 124–5, 137.
5. Ibid., p. 125.
6. Mitsui and Company, *The 100 Year History of Mitsui & Co. Ltd, 1876–1976* (Tokyo: Mitsui, 1977), pp. 158–9.
7. Ibid., pp. 169–70.
8. Mitsui Bank, *The Mitsui Bank*, op. cit., pp. 127–9.
9. Ibid., p. 129.
10. Ibid., p. 133.
11. Mitsui Bank, 'Directives on Loan Screening from the 10th Branch Managers' Meeting', in 'Records of Mitsui Bank's Branch Managers' Meetings' (unpublished).
12. Mitsui Bank, *The Mitsui Bank*, op. cit., p. 124.
13. Mitsui Bank, 'Directives on Foreign Exchange Operations from the 5th Branch Managers' Meeting', in 'Records of Mitsui Bank's Branch Managers' Meetings' (unpublished).
14. Kosei Torihiki Iinkai Jimukyoku (Executive Office, Fair Trade Commission) (ed.), *Saihensei Katei ni aru Boekishosha no Kihondoko* (Basic Trend of the Trading Companies' Reorganization) (Tokyo: Kosei Torihiki Kyokai, 1955), pp. 34–8.
15. Mitsui and Company, *The 100 Year History*, op. cit., p. 13.
16. Ibid., pp. 188–9.
17. 'The Three Main Companies' Consolidation on the Way to Mitsui & Co.'s Reestablishment: Memoirs of a former executive of Mitsui Bank' (unpublished manuscript).
18. Mitsui Bank, *The Mitsui Bank*, op. cit., pp. 122–3.
19. Mitsui Bank, 'Directives on Loan Screening from the 10th Branch Managers' Meeting', in 'Records of Mitsui Bank's Branch Managers' Meetings' (unpublished).
20. Fuji Bank, *The 100 Year History*, op. cit., pp. 802–5.
21. Mitsui Bank, 'Directives on Loan Screening', op. cit.
22. Fuji Bank, *The 100 Year History*, op. cit., pp. 928–9; Sanwa Bank, *Sanwa Ginko no Rekishi* (The History of Sanwa Bank) (Osaka: Sanwa Bank, 1974), pp. 407–30.
23. Mitsui Bank, 'Directives on Loan Screening from the 14th Branch Managers' Meeting', in 'Records of Mitsui Bank's Branch Managers' Meetings' (unpublished).
24. Ibid.
25. Mitsui Bank, 'Directives on Loan Screening from the 15th Branch Managers' Meeting', in 'Records of Mitsui Bank's Branch Managers' Meetings' (unpublished).
26. Mitsui Bank, 'Directives on Loan Screening from the 18th Managers' Meeting', in 'Records of Mitsui Bank's Branch Managers' Meetings' (unpublished).
27. Mitsui Bank, 'Directives on Loan Screening from the 15th Branch Managers' Meeting', op. cit.

28. Mitsui Bank, *The Mitsui Bank*, op. cit., pp. 135–6.
29. Ibid., p. 143.
30. Mitsui Bank, 'Directives on Foreign Exchange Operations from the 19th Branch Managers' Meeting', in 'Records of Mitsui Bank's Branch Managers' Meetings' (unpublished).
31. Mitsui and Company, *The 100 Year History*, op. cit., pp. 210–11.
32. About the banks' policy shift, please see Sanwa Bank, *Sanwa Ginko no Rekishi*, op. cit., pp. 414–15. Sanwa succeeded in 'cropping fruit' such as Hitachi and Toyota Motors.

5 Supplementary Devices to Win the Lending Battle

1. Fuji Bank, *Fuji Bank 1880–1980* (Tokyo: Fuji Bank, 1980), pp. 32–9.
2. These descriptions are drawn from the following: Mitsui Bank, *The Mitsui Bank: A History of the First 100 Years* (Tokyo: Mitsui Bank, 1976), pp. 141–2; Takufusa Nakamura, *A History of Showa Japan, 1926–1989* (Tokyo: University of Tokyo Press, 1998), p. 370; Fuji Bank, *The 100 Year History of Fuji Bank* (Tokyo: Fuji Bank, 1982), pp. 921–3, 963–4.
3. Mitsui Bank, *The Mitsui Bank*, op. cit., pp. 143–4, 149.
4. Fuji Bank, *The 100 Year History*, op. cit., pp. 925–6.
5. Sanwa Bank, *Sanwa ginko no Rekishi* (The History of Sanwa Bank) (Osaka: Sanwa Bank, 1974), pp. 416–17.
6. Ibid., pp. 418, 422, 471–2.
7. Industrial Bank of Japan, *Nihon Kogyo Ginko 75-nen Shi* (The 75 Year History of the Industrial Bank of Japan) (Tokyo: Industrial Bank of Japan, 1982), pp. 199, 204.
8. Ibid., p. 341.
9. Ibid., p. 341.
10. Ibid., p. 336.
11. Ibid., pp. 331–2.
12. Toru Oishi, *Fuyo Gurupu* (The Fuyo Group) (Tokyo: Yunion Shuppansha, 1975), pp. 39–98.
13. Industrial Bank of Japan, *Nihon Kogyo Ginto*, op. cit., p. 525.
14. Ibid., pp. 476–9.
15. Takuji Komiyama, *Nihon Chusho Kogyo Kenkyu* (A Study of Small and Medium-Sized Industries in Japan) (Tokyo: Chuo Koronsha, 1941), pp. 41–3.
16. Tsusho Sangyo Sho Sangyo Kozo Chosakai (The Industrial Structure Investigation Committee, MITI), *Nihon no Sangyo Kozo* (The Structure of Industry in Japan), vol. 3 (Tokyo: Tsusho Sangyo Kenkyusha, 1964), p. 480.
17. Shintaro Hayashi, *Nihon Kikai Yushutsu Ron* (On the Export of Machines from Japan) (Tokyo: Toyo Keizai Shimposha, 1961), p. iv.
18. Ibid., p. 270.
19. The Industrial Structure Investigation Committee, *Nihon no Sangyo Kozo*, op. cit., p. 490.

20. The Small and Medium Enterprise Agency, *1980-nendo Chushokigyo Hakusho* (White Paper on Small and Medium Enterprises for the 1980 Fiscal Year) (Tokyo: Ministry of Finance, 1981), p. 348.
21. Industrial Bank of Japan, *The 75 Year History*, op. cit., pp. 456, 678.
22. Shinji Ogura, *Kikai Kogyo to Shitaukesei* (The Subcontracting System in the Japanese Machinery Industry) (Tokyo: Sembundo, 1994), pp. 101–10.
23. Industrial Bank of Japan, *The 75 Year History*. op. cit., p. 677.
24. Huang Xio Chun, *Senmonshosha kara Sogoshosha e – Marubeni ni okeru Jirei Kenkyu* (From a Specialist Trader to a General Trader – a case study of Marubeni Corp.) (Kyoto: Rinsen Shoten, 1992), pp. 20, 97–8.
25. Ibid.

6   Dashing into Long-Term Capital Lending

1. Mitsui and Company, *The 100 Year History of Mitsui & Co. Ltd. 1876–1976* (Tokyo: Mitsui, 1977), pp. 230–1.
2. Ibid., pp. 214–21.
3. Mitsui Bank, *The Mitsui Bank: A History of the First 100 Years* (Tokyo: Mitsui Bank, 1976), p. 176.
4. Ibid., p. 164.
5. Ibid., pp. 177–8.
6. Ibid., pp. 188–9.
7. Nissan Motor Corporation, *Nissan Jidosha Shashi: 1964–1973* (The History of Nissan Motor Corporation: 1964–1973) (Tokyo: Nissan, 1975), p. 32.
8. Industrial Bank of Japan, *The 75 Year History of the Industrial Bank of Japan* (Tokyo: Industrial Bank of Japan, 1982), pp. 679–80.
9. Ibid.
10. Ibid., p. 678.
11. Ibid., p. 722.
12. Ibid., p. 709.
13. Ibid., p. 854.
14. Ibid., p. 727.
15. Takuji Matsuzawa, *Watashi no Ginko Showashi* (My Life in a Bank in the Showa Period) (Tokyo: Toyo Keizai Shimposha, 1985), pp. 128–32.
16. Fuji Bank, *The 100 Year History of Fuji Bank* (Tokyo: Fuji Bank, 1982), pp. 1038–40.
17. Industrial Bank of Japan, *The 75 Year History*, op. cit., p. 866.
18. Mitsui Bank, *The Mitsui Bank*, op. cit., pp. 162–3.
19. Takafusa Nakamura, *A History of Showa Japan, 1926–1989* (Tokyo: Tokyo University Press, 1998), p. 406.
20. Mitsui Bank, *The Mitsui Bank*, op. cit., p. 178.
21. Nakamura, *A History*, op. cit., p. 407.

Bibliography

Books and articles

Abe, Etsuo and Robert Fitzgerald (eds) (1995) *The Origins of Japanese Industrial Power* (London: Frank Cass).

Ando, Yoshio (1965–66) *Showa Keizaishi eno Shogen* (Testimonies to the Economic History of Showa) (Tokyo: Mainichi Shimbunsha).

Aoki, Masahiko and Hugh Patrick (eds) (1994) *The Japanese Main Bank System: Its Relevance for Developing and Transforming Economies* (New York: Oxford University Press).

Asahi Keizai Nenshi (The Asahi Economic Chronicle) (1932) (Osaka: Asahi Shimbunsha).

Asai, Yoshio (1977) 'Senkyuhyakuniju-nendai ni okeru Mitsui Ginko to Mitsui Zaibatsu' (Mitsui Bank and Mitsui Zaibatsu in the 1920s), Mitsui Bunko Ronso, no. 11 (Tokyo: Mitsui Research Institute for Social and Economic History).

Asajima, Shoichi (ed.) (1987) *Zaibatsu Kinyu Kozo no Hikakukenkyu* (A Comparative Study of the Financial Structure of Zaibatsu) (Tokyo: Ochanomizu Shobo).

Bank of Japan (1982–86) *Nihon Ginko 100-nen Shi* (A Hundred Year History of the Bank of Japan) (Tokyo: Bank of Japan).

Bank of Japan, Research Division (1974) *Nihon Kinyushi Shiryo; Showa Hen* (Materials on Japan's Financial History, the Showa Period), vol. 34 (Tokyo: Ministry of Finance).

Calder, Kent E. (1993) *Strategic Capitalism: private business and public purpose in Japanese industrial finance* (Princeton, NJ: Princeton University Press).

Chandler, Alfred D. Jr (1990) *Scale and Scope: the dynamics of industrial capitalism* (Cambridge, Mass.: Harvard University Press).

Chun, Huang Xio (1992) *Senmonshosha kara Sogoshosha e: Marubeni ni okeru Jirei Kenkyu* (From a Specialist Trader to a General Trader: a case study of Marubeni Corp.) (Kyoto: Rinsen Shoten).

Chushokigyo Cho (Small and Medium Enterprise Agency) (1981) *1980-nendo Chushokigyo Hakusho* (White Paper on Small and Medium-Sized Enterprises for the 1980 Fiscal Year) (Tokyo: Ministry of Finance).

Clark, Kim B. and Takahiro Fujimoto (1991) *Product Development Performance* (Boston, Mass. Harvard Business School Press).

Cohen, Jerome B. (1949) *Japan's Economy in War and Reconstruction* (Minneapolis: University of Minnesota Press).

Dai-Ichi Bank (1958) *Dai-Ichi Ginkoshi Gekan* (The History of Dai-Ichi Bank) part 2 (Tokyo: Dai-Ichi Bank).

Dore, Ronald P. (1986) *Flexible Rigidities: Industrial Policy and Structural Adjustment in the Japanese Economy 1970–80* (Stanford, CA: Stanford University Press).

Ekonomisuto Henshubu (ed.) (1979) *Sengo Sangyoshi eno Shogen, (5) Kigyo Shudan* (Testimonies to the Industrial History during the Postwar Years, part 5, Business Groups) (Tokyo: Mainichi Shimbunsha).

Ekonomisuto Henshubu (ed.) (1984) *Shogen, Kodo Seichoki no Nihon* (Testimonies to Japan's High-Speed Economic Growth) (Tokyo: Mainichi Shimbunsha).

Fuji Bank, (1960) *Fuji Ginko 80-nen Shi* (The 80 Year History of Fuji Bank) (Tokyo: Fuji Bank).

Fuji Bank (1980) *FUJI BANK 1880–1980* (English edition) (Tokyo: Fuji Bank).

Fuji Bank (1982) *Fuji Ginko 100-nen Shi* (The 100 Year History of Fuji Bank) (Tokyo: Fuji Bank).

Genther, Phyllis (1990) *A History of Japan's Government–Business Relationship: The Passenger Car Industry* (Ann Arbor, Mich. Center for Japanese Studies, University of Michigan).

Go, Tian-Kang (1971) *America Kinyushihon Seiritsushi* (The Evolution of Finance Capital in America, 1873–1914) (Tokyo: Yuhikaku).

Go, Tian-Kang (1999) *American Commercial Banks in Corporate Finance 1929–1941: A Study in Banking Concentration* (New York and London: Garland).

Goto, Shinichi (1970) *Nihon no Kinyu Tokei* (Financial Statistics of Japan) (Tokyo: Toyo Keizai Shimposha).

Goto, Shinichi (1977) *Futsu Ginko no Rinen to Genjitsu* (Commercial Banking in Japan: Images and Realities) (Tokyo: Toyo Keizai Shimposha).

Hagiwara, Tametsugu (1932) *Suppadaka ni shita Koshu Zaibatsu* (The Naked Truth About the Koshu Zaibatsu) (Tokyo: Tametsugu Hagiwara).

Hashimoto, Juro (1984) *Daikyokoki no Nihon Shihonshugi* (Japan's Capitalism during the Great Depression) (Tokyo: University of Tokyo Press).

Hashimoto, Juro and Haruhito Takeda (eds) (1992) *Nihon Keizai no Hatten to Kigyo Shudan* (Corporate Groupings in the Developing Japanese Economy) (Tokyo: University of Tokyo Press).

Hayashi, Shintaro (1961) *Nihon Kikai Yushutsu Ron* (On the Export of Machines from Japan) (Tokyo: Toyo Keizai Shimposha).

Ikeda, Seihin (1949) *Zaikai Kaiko* (Memoirs of the Japanese Business Circle) (Tokyo: Sekai no Nihonsha).

Imuta, Toshimitsu (ed.) (1991) *Senjitaiseika no Kinyu Kozo* (Financial Structure in War) (Tokyo: Nihon Hyoronsha).

Industrial Bank of Japan (1957) *Nihon Kogyo Ginko 50-nen Shi* (The 50 Year History of the Industrial Bank of Japan) (Tokyo: Industrial Bank of Japan).

Industrial Bank of Japan (1982) *Nihon Kogyo Ginko 75-nen Shi* (The 75 Year History of the Industrial Bank of Japan) (Tokyo: Industrial Bank of Japan).

Inoue Junnosuke Den (The Life of Junnosuke Inoue) (1935) (Tokyo: Inoue Junnosuke Ronso Hensankai).

Johnson, Chalmers (1982) *MITI and the Japanese Miracle: The Growth of Industrial Policy, 1925–1975* (Stanford, CA: Stanford University Press).

Kasuya, Makoto (1987) 'Nakamigawa Nyuko zengo no Mitsui Ginko' (The Consolidation of Loans and Reorganization of Mitsui Bank around 1890), *Keiei Shigaku*, vol. 22, no. 3.

Kasuya, Makoto (1990) 'Ginko no Zaibatsu ni taisuru Tokatsu-Mitsui Ginko no Jirei' (How Zaibatsu Controlled the Bank – the Case of Mitsui), *Keiei Shigaku*, vol. 24, no. 4.

Kato, Toshihiko (1957) *Hompo Ginkoshiron* (History of Japan's Banking) (Tokyo: University of Tokyo Press).

Keiretsu no Kenkyu (Research into Corporate Groupings) (various editions) (Tokyo: Keizai Chosa Kyokai).

Kigyo Keiretsu Soran (Yearbook on Corporate Groupings) (various editions) (Tokyo: Toyo Keizai Shimposha).

Kikkawa, Takeo (1995) *Nihon Denryokugyo no Hatten to Matsunaga Yasuzaemon* (The Development of Japan's Electric Power Industry and Yasuzaemon Matsunaga) (Nagoya: Nagoya Daigaku Shuppankai).

Komiyama, Takuji (1941) *Nihon Chusho Kogyo Kenkyu* (A Study of Small and Medium-Sized Industries in Japan) (Tokyo: Chuo Koronsha).

Kosei Torihiki Iinkai Jimukyoku (Executive Office, Fair Trade Commission) (ed.) (1955) *Saihensei Katei ni aru Boekishosha no Kihondoko* (Basic Trend of the Trading Companies' Reorganization) (Tokyo: Kosei Torihiki Kyokai).

Kyuno, Masao (1994) *Nihon no Toshiginko no Kenkyu* (A Study of Japan's Major Commercial Banks) (Tokyo: Chuo Keizaisha).

Matsumoto, Hiroshi (1979) *Mitsui Zaibatsu no Kenkyu* (A Study of the Mitsui Zaibatsu) (Tokyo: Yoshikawa Kobunkan).

Matsuzawa, Takuji (1985) *Watashi no Ginko Showashi* (My Life in a Bank in the Showa Period) (Tokyo: Toyo Keizai Shimposha).

Ministry of Finance (1976) *Showa Zaiseishi: Shusen kara Kowa made, vol. 12 Kinyu (1)* (Financial History of Showa: War's End to Peace Treaty, Finance, part. 1) (Tokyo: Toyo Keizai Shimposha).

Ministry of Finance (1983) *Showa Zaiseishi: Shusen kara Kowa made, vol. 13 Kinyu (2)* (Financial History of Showa, War's End to Peace Treaty, Finance, part. 2) (Tokyo: Toyo Keizai Shimposha).

Ministry of Finance (1991a) *Showa Zaiseishi: Showa 27-nendo kara 48-nendo made, vol. 9 Kinyu (1)* (Financial History of Showa: fiscal year 1952 to fiscal year 1973, Finance, part 1) (Tokyo: Toyo Keizai Shimposha).

Ministry of Finance (1991b) *Showa Zaiseishi: Showa 27-nendo kara 48-nendo made, vol. 10 Kinyu (2)* (Financial History of Showa: fiscal year 1952 to fiscal year 1973, Finance, part 2) (Tokyo: Toyo Keizai Shiomposha).

Ministry of International Trade and Industry (MITI) (1961, 1972) *Shoko Seisakushi* (History of the Ministry's Industrial and Commercial Policies), vols 9 and 10 (Tokyo: MITI).

Mishima, Yasuo (1989) *The Mitsubishi: its challenge and strategy* (Greenwich, Conn.: Jai Press).

Mitsubishi Bank (1954) *Mitsubishi Ginkoshi* (The History of Mitsubishi Bank) (Tokyo: Mitsubishi Bank).

Mitsubishi Corporation (1986) *Mitsubishi Shoji Shashi* (The History of Mitsubishi Corp.) (Tokyo: Mitsubishi).

Mitsubishi Economic Research Institute (1955) *Mitsui, Mitsubishi and Sumitomo: Present Status of the Former Zaibatsu Enterprises* (Tokyo: Mitsubishi Economic Research Institute).

Mitsui and Company (1977) *The 100 Year History of Mitsui & Co., Ltd, 1876–1976* (Tokyo: Mitsui).

Mitsui Bank (1957) *Mitsui Ginko 80-nen Shi* (The 80 Year History of Mitsui Bank) (Tokyo: Mitsui Bank).

Mitsui Bank (1976) *The Mitsui Bank; A History of the First 100 Years* (English edition) (Tokyo: Mitsui Bank).

Mitsui Family Council (Mitsuike Dozokukai) (1973–76) 'Mitsuike Dozokukai Kanribu Kaigiroku' (The Minutes of the Council's Control Department), *Mitsui Bunko Ronso*, nos 7–10 (Tokyo: Mitsui Research Institute for Social and Economic History).

Morikawa, Hidemasa (1980) *Zaibatsu no Keieishiteki Kenkyu* (Studies in the Business History of the Zaibatsu) (Tokyo: Toyo Keizai Shimposha).

Morikawa, Hidemasa (1992) *Zaibatsu: the rise and fall of family enterprise groups in Japan* (Tokyo: University of Tokyo Press).

Moroo, Seiji (1940) *Jigyo Kinyu Jimbutsu: Daido Denryoku 20-nen Kinyushi Kou* (Business, Finance and Leading Figures: A Study of Daido Electric Power Co.'s Capital Raising over 20 Years) (Nishinomiya, Hyogo Prefecture: Seiji Moroo).

MRISEH (1971–74) (ed.) *Mitsui Jigyoshi Shiryohen* (Historical Materials for the History of Mitsui Business Enterprises), parts 3–4 (Tokyo: Mitsui Research Institute for Social and Economic History).

MRISEH (1980–84) *Mitsui Jigyo Shi* (The History of Mitsui Business Enterprises), vols 2–3 (Tokyo: Mitsui Research Institute for Social and Economic History).

Nakamura, Takafusa (1998) *A History of Showa Japan, 1926–1989* (Tokyo: University of Tokyo Press).

Narita, Kiyohide (1958) *Oji Seishi Shashi* (History of the Oji Paper) (Tokyo: Oji Paper).

Nihon Keieishi Kenkyusho (1969) *Nakamigawa Hikojiro Denki Shiryo* (Biographical Materials on Hikojiro Nakamigawa) (Tokyo: Toyo Keizai Shimposha).

Nihon Keieishi Kenkyusho (Japan Business History Institute, JBHI) (ed.) (1977–78) *Mitsui Ginko Shiryo* (Historical Materials on Mitsui Bank), parts 2–5 (Tokyo: JBHI).

Nishiguchi, Toshihiro (1994) *Strategic Industrial Sourcing: the Japanese advantage* (New York: Oxford University Press).

Nissan Motors (1975) *Nissan Jidosha Shashi: 1964–1973* (The History of Nissan Motors: 1964–1973) (Tokyo: Nissan Motors).

Ogura, Shinji (1990) *Senzenki Mitsui Ginko Kigyotorihiki Kankeishi no Kenkyu* (Mitsui Bank and its Customers, 1900–1943) (Tokyo: Sembundo).

Oishi, Toru (1975) *Fuyo Gurupu* (The Fuyo Group) (Tokyo: Yunion Shuppansha).

Okazaki, Tetsuji and Masahiro Okuno-Fujiwara (eds) (1993) *Gendai Nihon Keizai Shisutemu no Genryu* (Historical Origins of the Contemporary Japanese Economic System) (Tokyo: Nihon Keizai Shimbunsha).

Okimoto, Daniel I. (1989) *Between MITI and the Market* (Stanford, CA: Stanford University Press).

Okumura, Hiroshi (1975) *Hojin Shihonshugi no Kozo* (The Structure of Corporate Capitalism) (Tokyo: Nihon Hyoronsha).

Roberts, John G. (1989) *Mitsui: three centuries of Japanese business*, 2nd edn (New York: Weatherhill).

Saito, Hisahiko (1981) *Kinhoniseika no Zaigai Seika* (The Specie Held Abroad under the Gold Standard) (Tokyo: The United Nations University).

Sanwa Bank (1974) *Sanwa Ginko no Rekishi* (The History of Sanwa Bank) (Osaka: Sanwa Bank).

Sasaki, Kuni (ed.) (1964) *Arishihi Hitotoshite no Mandai Junshiro* (The Life of Junshiro Mandai and His Personality) (Yokosuka: Toshi Mandai).

Sato, Kiichiro (1962) *Ori ni Furete* (My Reminiscences), part 2 (Tokyo: Institute for Banking and Financial Research).

Sato, Sadayuki (1984) *Takokuseki Kigyo no Seijikeizaigaku* (The Political Economy of Multinational Enterprises) (Tokyo: Yuhikaku).

Shibagaki, Kazuo (1965) *Nihon Kinyushihon Bunseki* (An Analysis of Finance Capital in Japan) (Tokyo: University of Tokyo Press).

Shimada, Katsumi (1986) *Shosha Shoken Ron* (Traders' Commercial Rights) (Tokyo: Toyo Keizai Shimposha).

Sumitomo Bank (1979) *Sumitomo Ginko 80-nen Shi* (The 80 Year History of Sumitomo Bank) (Osaka: Sumitomo Bank).

Suzuki, Ken (1998) *Mein Banku to Kigyo Shudan* (Main Banks and Corporate Groupings) (Kyoto: Minerva Shobo).

Takeda, Haruhito (ed.) (1995) *Nihon Sangyo Hatten no Dainamizumu* (The Dynamism of Developing Japanese Industry) (Tokyo: University of Tokyo Press).

Teranishi, Juro (1982) *Nihon no Keizai Hatten to Kinyu* (Japanese Economic Development and Financial System) (Tokyo: Iwanami Shoten).

Tokyo Electric Light Company (1936) *Tokyo Dento Kabushiki Kaisha Kaigyo 50-nen Shi* (The 50 Year History of Tokyo Electric Light Co.) (Tokyo: Tokyo Electric Light Co.)

Toshiba (1940) *Shibaura Seisakusho 65-nen Shi* (The 65 Year History of Shibaura Electric Works) (Tokyo: Toshiba).

Tsusho Sangyo Sho Sangyo Kozo Chosakai (The Industrial Structure Investigation Committee, MITI) (1964) *Nihon no Sangyo Kozo* (The Structure of Industry in Japan), vol. 3 (Tokyo: Tsusho Sangyo Kenkyusha).

US Senate Committee on Finance (1931–32) *Sale of Foreign Bonds or Securities in the United States* (Washington, DC: Government Printing Office).

Wada, Kazuo (1991) 'The Development of Tiered Inter-Firm Relationships in the Automobile Industry: A Case Study of Toyota Motor Corporation', in Business Society of Japan (ed.), *Japanese Year Book on Business History*, vol. 8 (Tokyo: University of Tokyo Press).

Yamazaki, Hiroaki (1979) 'Senjika no Sangyo Kozo to Dokusen Soshiki' (Industrial Structure and Monopolistic Organizations during the War), in University of Tokyo, Social Science Research Institute (ed.), *Fashizumuki no Kokka to Shakai, vol. 2: Senji Nippon Keizai* (State and Society under Fascism: Japan's Economy in War) (Tokyo: University of Tokyo Press).

Yamazaki, Hiroaki (1992) 'The Yokohama Specie Bank during the period of the restored gold standard in Japan (January 1930–December 1931)', in Youssef Cassis (ed.), *Finance and financiers in European history, 1880–1960* (Cambridge: Cambridge University Press).

Yoneyama Umekichi Den (The Life of Umekichi Yoneyama) (1960) (Tokyo: Aoyama Gakuin Shotobu).

Yui, Tsunehiko (ed.) (1986) *Yasuda Zaibatsu* (The Yasuda Zaibatsu) (Tokyo: Nihon Keizai Shimbunsha).

Unpublished documents

'Collected Directives from Teikoku Bank's Head Office' parts 1 and 2 (Sakura Bank archives – Sakura in April 2001 merged with Sumitomo Bank and became the Sumitomo Mitsui Banking Corporation).

'Documents on Teikoku Bank's Operations' (Sakura Bank archives).

'Memoirs of ex-Executives of Mitsui Bank' (Sakura Bank archives).

Mitsui and Company 'Minutes of the 8th Branch Managers' Meeting' (Mitsui Research Institute for Social and Economic History [hereafter MRISEH] archives).

Mitsui and Company, 'Minutes of the 10th Branch Managers' Meeting' (MRISEH archives).

Mitsui and Company, 'Semi-Annual Reports for 1917' (MRISEH archives).

Mitsui Bank, 'Documents on the Bank's Large Substantial Credit to Customers' (Sakura Bank archives).

Mitsui Bank, 'Directives from the Head Office' (Sakura Bank archives).

Mitsui Bank, 'Records of Mitsui Bank's Branch Managers' Meetings'.

Mitsui Bank, 'Semi-annual Reports to the Mitsui Gomei' (Sakura Bank's archives).

Mitsui Bank, 'Audit Report for the First Quarter of 1943' (Sakura Bank archives).

Mitsui Bank, 'Collected Chairman's Addresses to Branch Managers' Meetings' (Sakura Bank archives).

Mitsui Bank, 'Minutes of the Board of Directors' (Sakura Bank archives).

Mitsui Bank, 'Minutes of General Managers' Meetings' (Sakura Bank archives).

Mitsui Bank, Supplement to the Hochi (the bank's internal newspaper) (Sakura Bank archives).

Mitsui Bank, New York Branch, 'Report on an Investigation into Investment Bankers, 1925' (Sakura Bank archives).

The Secret Story of and Documents on Mitsui Bank, 4 vols (Sakura Bank archives).

'Three Main Companies' Consolidation on the Way to Mitsui & Co.'s Reestablishment' memoirs of former executive of Mitsui Bank (privately owned manuscript).

Index